ADVANCE PRAISE FOR FROM APOSTLE TO APOSTATE

"In this fascinating volume, part personal memoir, part social commentary, Catherine Dunphy shines a light on one of the most complex and understudied phenomena of our secularising age— the plight of once-believing but now nonbelieving clergy. The results are impossible to put down."

—Andrew Copson, Chief Executive, British Humanist Association

"Many years ago I struggled with a debilitating form of panic disorder. Finally I was lucky enough to listen to a recording of others who suffered from the same, recovered, and were brave enough to share their stories. Instantly my life changed for the better. In a moment I learned that I was not alone and that I was not flawed. This book and Catherine's story in particular will give many that same depth of relief, along with a true sense of belonging and peace of mind! She assures us that we're not alone nor are we flawed. Her story is captivating, the language is pure poetry, and the resulting insights are life changing . . . life enhancing. Consider yourself lucky for reading this book."

—Jerry DeWitt, author of *Hope After Faith: An Ex-Pastor's Journey from Belief to Atheism*

"I love the blend of the scholarly and the personal in Catherine Dunphy's *From Apostle to Apostate*. This fascinating account of what happens when clergy embrace reason and abandon faith comes with dizzyingly high stakes and life-altering revelations. A former clergyperson myself, I resonate with the truths on every page. Deftly written and bravely told, *From Apostle to Apostate* deserves a wide reading and is sure to provoke lively discussion."

—Mary Johnson, author of *An Unquenchable Thirst: A Memoir*

"As someone intimately involved in developing the Clergy Project, I thought I knew everything about it, so I was surprised and delighted to find new insights in Catherine Dunphy's *From Apostle to Apostate*. I love the way she interweaves the story of the Clergy Project and personal insights from its members with religious philosophy and her own experiences with Roman Catholicism. The cleverly placed Bible quotes are a nice touch. Her Jesuit education has found a useful expression in this book beyond anything she or the theologians who taught her ever could have imagined."

—Linda LaScola, coauthor, with Daniel C. Dennett, of *Caught in the Pulpit: Leaving Belief Behind*

"It's never easy to reveal a secret. To do so when it could turn your life upside-down and possibly alienate everyone you love is a tremendous act of courage. Catherine Dunphy went through that difficult journey. Through her work with the Clergy Project and in *From Apostle to Apostate*, she helps us all navigate that world. Whether you're a pastor or a teenager living in the Bible Belt, Dunphy reminds those who doubt the existence of God that they're not alone."

—Hemant Mehta, editor of FriendlyAtheist.com

"Not all clergy are slick evangelists or abusers of children. Many entered the ministry with a sincere and hopeful desire to promote truth and meet human needs. But now some of them, for the same reasons, have stepped away. Catherine Dunphy is one of those caring and intelligent ministers who no longer believes in the supernatural and has found her way out. Her warmth and insight will help others make the same painful but honest transition from apostle to apostate."

—Dan Barker, copresident of the Freedom From Religion Foundation and author of *Life Driven Purpose: How an Atheist Finds Meaning*

FROM APOSTLE TO APOSTATE

The Story of the Clergy Project

Catherine Dunphy

Foreword by Richard Dawkins

PITCHSTONE PUBLISHING
Durham, North Carolina

Pitchstone Publishing
Durham, North Carolina
www.pitchstonepublishing.com

Copyright © 2015 by Catherine Dunphy

10 9 8 7 6 5 4 3 2 1

Library of Congress Cataloging-in-Publication Data

Dunphy, Catherine, 1973- author.
  From apostle to apostate : the story of the Clergy Project / Catherine
Dunphy ; Foreword by Richard Dawkins.
    pages cm
  ISBN 978-1-63431-016-1 (paperback)
  1. Clergy Project. 2. Ex-clergy. 3. Christianity and atheism. I. Title.
  BL2747.D86 2015
  206'.1—dc23
                                                    2014042523

for Rowan

Prostrate

The bones of ancient grottos,
*   mixed with seasons spent excavating crumbling meaning.*
Cloistered and confident in delusion,
The rhythmic hum of convictions buttressed by want and need.

Our common yearning for shared significance,
*   falling short and failing happiness.*
Call and response, the melodic overture of self-sacrifice,
The thrill of breaking rules, the guilt of pleasure.

The warm embrace of identity loss,
The stilling of my mind,
The silencing of individuality.

Unwarranted holiness.
A drink from a well, that runs too deep.

—Catherine Dunphy (2014)

If I speak of life and of the universe, and am not in awe, then I have no humility and have failed to grasp the beauty of reality, and my own insignificance. And if I have acquired knowledge and used these skills to ask questions, and to understand the mysteries of life and of the universe, but am not in awe, then I am obfuscating.

Awe is love; awe is reciprocity; awe is motivating. It does not insist on its own way; its only goal is to communicate meaning; it is not irritable or resentful; it does not take sides, but rejoices in the truth.

As for prophecies, their time has come to an end; as for faith in supernaturalism, it too will wane; we are learning. The urge for innovation will help us make new discoveries, about our planet, our universe, and ourselves.

When I was a child, I thought and spoke like a child, my reasoning was limited. Now I am an adult, I have put an end to childish methods and have embraced reality.

Awe stirs us from our isolated slumber, to see the world clearly, and to share this knowledge, caretaking it for future generations.

—Catherine Dunphy (2014), inspired by 1 Corinthians 1–13

Apostate

*noun, a person who renounces a religious
or political belief or principle.*

*Middle English: from ecclesiastical Latin apostate;
origin Greek apostatēs 'apostate, runaway slave'.*

—Oxford English Dictionary

CONTENTS

FOREWORD

This beautifully written book, the testament of a sensitive, empathetic and highly intelligent woman, is in part a deeply moving personal memoir, in part an essential source document for future histories of the Clergy Project. As she recounts, the Clergy Project has long been a dream of several of us in the secular movement. It was born of sympathy for the unique predicament of clergymen and women who find themselves "caught in the pulpit" (title of Dan Dennett and Linda LaScola's book on the subject). The farmer who tires of the land, the accountant who aspires to the law, the businesswoman who longs to be a doctor, the army officer who dreams of a schoolteaching vocation, all these face financial hardship and an uphill struggle to retrain, and master new skills. But their exit plan doesn't additionally put them at risk of losing friends, family, and respect in their community with the bruising danger—unless they are very strong—of a knock-on loss of self-respect. But a priest, pastor or rabbi who, through the power of thought in the clear light of reason or the dark night of the soul, becomes an atheist, is in a uniquely vulnerable position. Catherine Dunphy's wrenching ordeal when her mother learned of her apostasy is all too typical. The malign power of childhood indoctrination seizes mothers, fathers, spouses, children, parishioners, neighbours: rouses them to ostracise, shun, banish into loneliness the unfortunate victim whose only crime, when you face it coolly, is dispassionate and logical thinking. The lonely isolation comes on top of the financial hardship that can be expected to attend any change of career. The Clergy Project was set up to provide a refuge, a haven of sympathetic understanding, where apostate or progressively doubting clergy could find each other, talk to each other in the safety of often pseudonymous anonymity, maybe even cry on each other's virtual shoulders: a confiding oasis where those already well advanced in their progress towards "coming out" could offer advice and succour to those beginning their upward path.

Catherine Dunphy was a founding member of the Clergy Project and one of the first to come out. She bears moving witness to the difficulties that face all her colleagues, now more than 600 strong, as they struggle, in their different ways, to come to terms with their loss of faith, and start to emerge into the light. The struggle is different in every case of course. Catherine testifies to the particular difficulties of being both a woman and a Roman Catholic, cradle votary of that singularly misogynistic and unbendingly hidebound institution. Her reluctance to leave, born of relentless brainwashing in childhood, led her to seek last ditch reconciliation with the church via "liberation theology" and "feminist theology". Such liberal apologists seem to have provided her with temporary respite before she finally realised that the problem was with theology itself. She finally gave up her faith altogether and experienced the unburdening lightness of relief that so many others, in their different ways, have encountered.

Her book includes revealing interviews with other members of the Clergy Project, some named, some still anonymous, all of whom have their own version of a similar story. One observes that coming out as atheist was far harder, and led to far more hurtful ill-treatment than coming out as gay. Through all these tetimonials I, as a scientist who lost faith because of the conspicuous failure of religion to explain the natural world, was struck by how many members of the Clergy Project travelled a different route. For them, disillusionment with the morals of their respective churches and the personal shortcomings of their priests, was paramount. They internally repudiated their church before they stopped believing in God. Catherine herself was especially disgusted by the behaviour of her Bishop, covering up and making light of the sexual abuse of children, while pulling outraged rank over those who questioned him—both particular vices of the Roman Catholic Church.

My own, probably over-hasty response to those people of faith who experience the hollowness of disillusionment is, "Why don't you just leave? After all there's no positive reason, not even the smallest grounds, for believing in the factual claims of your church. Now that you've perceived its moral feet of clay, why don't you just walk?" Catherine Dunphy has taught me that this is too dispassionately scientific, too briskly cold. Her intelligence shines a painfully revealing light on the tragedy of entrapment. Great is the power of childhood imprinting. Those who inflict it can be forgiven only because they themselves were the innocent victims of it in their own early and impressionable years. Correspondingly great is the courage and strength of character of those who rise above it and break the cycle, refusing to hand the scourge on to the next generation. Those who were unfortunate enough to take the additional step of commitment to a life career in the clergy deserve special sympathy and praise when they have the courage to leave.

Catherine Dunphy's book will serve to stiffen the resolve of those still in the closet—and the 600 who have so far joined the Clergy Project must surely be the tip of a large and still swelling iceberg. It will also serve as a warning to those who might otherwise have been lured—"called" as they would perhaps put it—into the blind alley of commitment to the career that she has thankfully renounced. The good things that clergy sometimes do—fostering good fellowship and community, charitable work, education of a nonreligious character—can be achieved in secular ways without supernatural nonsense and without dictatorial hierarchies. Here, as elsewhere, Catherine Dunphy serves as a role model, and her book as a beacon of hope.

—Richard Dawkins
Oxford, England

PROLOGUE

"I am the voice of one crying out in the wilderness."
—John 1:23

It is a truly radical experience for a clergyperson to admit that their beliefs, and the faith that they have long articulated, have lost their meaning. It is more than the dark night of the soul; it is the utter abandonment of a worldview that, after thorough study, reflection, and lived experience, fails to withstand critique both intellectually and emotionally. It is a revelation that uncomfortably exposes the internal architecture of self-delusion and the social and religious constructs that buttress these imaginative ideologies. It is a journey that all members of the Clergy Project have taken, myself included.

Founded in 2011 to help lift the sense of isolation uniformly noted by nonbelieving clergy in the landmark study by Daniel C. Dennett and Linda LaScola titled "Preachers Who Are Not Believers," the Clergy Project is the first organization dedicated to providing an opportunity for clergy to support one another through the challenges of working in ministry after having relinquished their faith. As one of the fifty-two original members of the Clergy Project, I have had the privilege of seeing the project emerge and grow. What started off as an idea has bloomed, within a few short years, into a vibrant community of more than six hundred members, hailing from every part of the world and representing every major world religion.

Each member brings with them a story of faith lost and of a life transformed. The similarities of these converging stories are very striking, and this commonality has allowed friendships to flourish as members recognize the value of being understood and heard. Like me, each member of the Clergy Project has put aside belief in an intercessory creator god and has found comfort in a more tangible reality—that life and existence, even if undirected by supernatural or magical influences, is nonetheless awe-inspiring and worthy of protecting. Our lives and the life that we share this planet with have value simply because we value it! To wax theological, we imbue life with the meaning we seek.

Religion has long claimed the right to name and interpret meaning, and as active and former religious leaders, I and the other members of the Clergy Project understand the power that religion holds over believers—how it encourages believers to tap into the emotion of life, saturating their senses with color, light, beauty, and significance. Religion is a great theatrical production, meant to catapult us past the so-called mundanities and limits of life into the intoxicating highs of the spirit. What religion and its advocates misunderstand, and what members of the Clergy Project have embraced, is that life is not mundane; it does not radiate sin. Life simply is, and religions' attempts to box it in and claim authority only devalues the beauty of reality and succeeds in making a mockery out of these so-called moral institutions. Despite the persuasiveness of religion, the religious narrative is an exceedingly temporary fix.

Though I now see clearly the limits of belief and the confines of faith, when I was a believer—a born and bred Roman Catholic—I too embraced the emotion of religion. It felt intuitive. The gore and glory of Catholicism are embodied in the religion's exhalation of the sacrament of the Eucharist, a fixation on pain, suffering, and redemption. This mentality encroached upon every aspect of my life as a believer. I was fully initiated into the rites and rituals of the Church. This spiritual education taught me a thing or two about theological pedagogy and the methods that the Church utilizes to engage its followers and to entice converts. I was baptized, received my holy communion, sought penance through reconciliation, and was confirmed. That indoctrination process took more than fifteen years. It should therefore come as no surprise that it took nearly as much time for me to transition from orthodox Catholic to liberal Catholic to atheist. My journey, though unique in its own way, is not exceptional. There are as many journeys from faith to reason as Clergy Project members. Although each journey is different from the next, we share common experiences and values.

We have each had a personal devotion to faith and have given our all to the vocation we chose—or, rather, were "called" for. In many cases, this meant sacrificing more lucrative employment opportunities and personal well-being, all to be part of something bigger.

We each went into ministry looking to find answers and meaning. I, for one, was wholeheartedly committed to the idea of helping to bring about the kingdom of God on earth by participating in good works. I thought at the time that studying theology would strengthen this commitment, by enabling me to better understand scripture and to more effectively communicate the gospel to those I ministered. I see now that much of this interest stemmed from my motivation to find answers to questions that had long troubled me and to quell my confusion when I read the Bible or asked questions of religious leaders.

We each saw ministry as an opportunity to do good work and to be of service to our communities. This desire to help has since extended outside of our religious traditions, as members who have left active ministry tend to gravitate toward helping professions, such as nonprofit service, social work, psychology, and governance.

We have each been willing to accept reality. For believers, doubt is the calling card of desolation. Overcoming this seemingly impassive obstacle defines the struggle of all clergy. Each member of the Clergy Project has gone through this process and—unlike other clergy who doubt but continue to believe—has rejected the idea of making a hasty retreat to faith.

We have each been tied to an ideology that sought principally to replicate adherence to its dogma. As fabricated as this sounds, such constructs are what kept me—and countless others—inside religion for so long. I capitulated my identity, values, and goals to a social organism whose only endeavor was self-replication. This process demands that clergy forgo their own well-being and happiness in order to sustain the unmoved and indifferent institutions that ensnare them.

Although we may have each rejected the fallacy and indoctrination of religion, we understand the desire to help and minister to others, and we know that communities often need help finding meaning during difficult times. We no longer rely on the formula that we previously used to interpret and articulate this meaning. Doing so would be similar to trying to follow a recipe when half the ingredients don't exist. Rather, we cultivate meaning in the reciprocity and reasoned deliberation of humanism.

As with other Clergy Project members, my own transition from a person of faith to a person of reason was not a short or thoughtless path. It took into account not only my theological education, but also the fabric of my culture and the expectations of my family. Faith was an intricate part of my life, something instilled and cultivated, in large part, by my mother. As a result, I was a "slow learner" when it came to giving up God. I railed against the doubt. Faith may require compromise, suspension of reason, and the acquiescing of judgment, but it offers the comfort of arrogant certainty and a millennia-old community from which to draw support.

Even so, ministry can be an exceedingly isolating experience, as the individual becomes annexed as a "holy person" or a "man/woman of God." Alienation is tricky in that much of it is internalized. The problem of burnout and depression among active clergy is so pervasive that many denominations institute policies and programs to help prevent or to even treat such conditions. For example, Roman Catholic priests are required to take annual spiritual retreats, as well as vacation time every year, and the Methodist Church has instituted a Clergy Health Initiative out of Duke University to assist its clergy coping with these wide-reaching challenges. The demands of keeping up with a congregation and its members' psychological and spiritual needs are draining at the best of times. When the minister, priest, rabbi, or imam also happens to be a nonbeliever, this stress level is multiplied. Not only are these individuals challenged by the external demands of meeting the emotional and spiritual needs of their place of worship, but they are also confronted by a powerful internal conflict—the schism between their public articulation of doctrinal beliefs and the simple fact that they are no longer believers.

Hiding in the atheist closet provides protection from judgment, protection from hostility, and protection of livelihood, but it does nothing to protect from this heightened sense of alienation. Until the founding of the Clergy Project, there was very little opportunity for faithless clergy to find support or a sympathetic ear. The protective boundary of anonymity that the Clergy Project provides nonbelieving religious leaders of every persuasion acts in many ways as a cloister. Inside the safety of our virtual walls, we are free to interact, to share our stories, and to find community. The project provides to clergy, for the first time, a sanctuary and a community of peers that provides not a place of worship, but rather, a place for reason, scrubbed clean of theism.

Although this book is about the Clergy Project, it is also about my own personal journey from faith to disbelief, as I draw extensively on my experiences and recollections to help tell the project's shared story through my own individual lens. Thus, much of the discussion revolves around the Roman Catholic Church and my evolving relationship with it, especially as a woman. Though a lot of what I share relates specifically to Catholicism and its teachings, the journey that I took—both from an emotional and intellectual standpoint— has parallels with the journeys taken by all members of the Clergy Project, no matter their past denomination or religion.

As with any extended journey or transformation, clear stages can be identified. I have thus divided this volume into three parts to suggest this idea.

The first part of the book examines the underlying need for the Clergy Project and the great anticipation with which the project's launch was met. I focus specifically on the sense of isolation, uncertainty, and fear experienced by nonbelieving clergy. I also shed light on the Clergy Project's foundation. In an effort to provide as complete a picture as possible, I interviewed each of the project's founders about the genesis of the project, their motivations for launching it, and their hopes for its future.

When I have an opportunity to speak about the project, I am often asked, "What is a typical Clergy Project member like?" and "Why did these clergy lose their faith?" The second part of the book answers these two questions—the first, with a quantitative examination of project membership, and the second, with a qualitative analysis of oft-stated factors that contributed to members' gradual erosion of faith. In many instances, these factors caused them to question authority and transform their values. They include the theological training clergy receive that is meant to inform their faith and ministry and challenges to their belief systems, particularly as relates to social justice issues, such as women's and LGBT rights.

The third part of the book looks at what project members have gained and lost in their journey from faith to disbelief, deals with the causes and consequences of a loss of faith, and discusses briefly the role clergy project members might play in the ongoing negotiation between faith and reason. It also demonstrates how many project members today articulate values and create meaning without a belief in God. Unlike faith traditions, these values do not claim a supernatural context; they are like all morals, mores, memes, and ethics—social constructs that have grown and morphed out of the social and biological history of our species. In many ways, we remain like our hunter-gatherer ancestors, attempting to not only survive the landscape, but also to make our mark upon it.

I am sure that the existence of the Clergy Project and the phenomenon of faithless religious leaders are unsettling to believers. They may interpret our rejection of faith in ways that give them comfort; they may say we are leaders who have lost our way; they may calls us troublemakers; or they may claim we have never been true believers, but the reality is that each member of the Clergy Project simply followed theology to its inevitable conclusions. This does not mean that our members do not see any benefit or good in religious communities—we do. We have simply accepted known reality. As our collective narrative shows, we may be considered apostates who have rejected faith and the supremacy of sacred literature, but we remain the same people who committed our lives to the values of compassion, ethics, and empathy and to our common humanity.

PART I
GENESIS: A PREHISTORY

1

LIVING IN ISOLATION

"He has put my family far from me,
and my acquaintances are wholly estranged from me."
—Job 19:13

Keeping a secret is an unintended exercise in loneliness that is fraught with fear, regret, and trepidation. For clergy who have shed their faith but who remain in the pulpit, this loneliness takes on a whole new dimension as they externally reiterate and promulgate religious ideologies that they have internally rejected. They do so for fear of repudiation from their communities and sanction by their denominational hierarchy. Even former clergy, whose options are generally better, are often unable to speak to trusted friends, family members, or allies regarding their loss of faith for like fears. As such, the stakes for nonbelieving clergy can be incredibly high. Depending upon their personal situation and circumstances, members of the Clergy Project face potential threats to their well-being, including physical violence, financial uncertainty, and broken relationships with family and friends. This is a difficult place to find yourself after you have committed so much time, effort, and energy to cultivating your vocation and serving your community.

In 2004 I graduated from Regis College at the University of Toronto with a Master of Theological Studies degree, but this was not what I had intended when I enrolled in seminary some years earlier. I had planned on completing a joint Master of Divinity and Master of Arts degree, with the goal of working in chaplaincy and pursuing a doctorate. My break from faith began to take hold after my second year as a Master of Divinity student. I had just wrapped up a heavy semester and was preparing to spend the summer working on my theological field placement, where I would provide pastoral care to a local community group supporting adult residents with developmental disabilities. I was excited about this opportunity to expand my experience in ministry beyond my earlier work running the Archdiocese of Halifax's Refugee Outreach Program. I had hoped that this placement would allow me to utilize my burgeoning pastoral skills.

I had heard mostly good things about the group I would be providing pastoral care for and its commitment to the ideals of social justice and living the gospel. Unfortunately, I noticed almost immediately a subverted hostility among the community workers, who had a propensity to idolize the residents, comparing their physical and emotional suffering to Christ. At the same time, they appeared to be competing with one another to see who was most committed to following the word of God. To complicate things further, many workers took part in detrimental off-duty group activities, such as binge drinking, which resulted in sexual impropriety and harassment. Collectively, this caused extreme tension among the workers. The level of dysfunction stunned me, and I was worried about the impact this corrosive environment might have on the people these workers were charged with caring for.

I attempted to raise my concerns with my supervisor but was advised not to intercede, and the limited attempts I made to minister to the individual workers failed, as my efforts were either misconstrued or misinterpreted and thus were unproductive. I left this post feeling disillusioned, not only with the level of impairment that religious ideology and magisterium had had on the well-being of these individuals and their interactions, but also with my own ability to effectively and successfully help people. Unhappy about this outcome, I recognized that I had been guilty of idealizing my religious community and that the major culprit was my own unrealistic expectations—and my growing doubt. I knew I would ultimately have one of two choices: to retreat into my idealized faith and disallow my doubt, or to embrace my doubt, a path fraught with the unknown, and accept that the tenets of my faith did not align with known reality.

My theological education provided me with the ability to conceptualize, visualize, construct, and manipulate a deity that suited my needs. This may have been an unintended consequence when I began my studies, but nonetheless these skills transformed my insight of God and forced me to acknowledge that he/she/it was just a scant projection of the internal values I had accumulated over years of religious assimilation.

In a rather expeditious fashion, I began to see my efforts in ministry as futile and disingenuous. I was forced to admit to myself that my beliefs had been hollowed out. As I attempted to align my religious narrative and my relentless doubt, I knew that I was perpetuating ideas and beliefs that had morphed away from church teaching and that I could no longer put my finger on what I believed. I attempted to keep up appearances, but my faith was shifting as fast as the sand on shore, and I did not like how that reflected on my personal integrity. I felt like a liar.

In true seminary fashion, I spoke with my theological adviser, who reminded me that no one could fully understand God—that we can only do our best to interpret him. She reminded me that the Church only gives us direction and that I would have to bring these challenges to God in prayer. This meeting did nothing more than lead me further to the despair that was slowly defining my religious life. I remember at the time mulling over a phrase from one of my classes, "Doubt is reasonable." I felt powerless to cease the endless questioning, to stop the never-ending litany of belief running through my head, and to have the emotion linked to my religion exorcised from my brain. I attempted to lay it out before me like a specimen to be studied, reviewed, and assessed—to deconstruct the certainty of which the Church, and we, and I spoke when we mentioned this thing called God—but I was fearful of the conclusions I might draw.

This long drawn-out process finally hit the harsh wall of reason while I listened to a lecture in my creation class. Thirty or so divinity students sat listening to our Jesuit professor pontificate on the radical accomplishments of Jesus. He was clearly excited about his attempt to blow our minds with the beauty of Christ's gift to creation when he asked us, "Did Jesus die for the gerbil?" The small classroom erupted with sporadic laughter, and puzzled faces looked at him, silently questing his sanity as we waited for someone to answer his absurd question. Eventually he answered, practically yelling,

"Well, yes, of course! Aren't gerbils a part of creation after all?" The pointlessness of his presentation angered me. Why was I sitting in a class being lectured on something so irrelevant and transparently artificial? I stopped listening to him and started to think, "Why was I studying theology anyway? Did I believe any of this? I heard a quiet response, 'no.'" I closed my eyes and let doubt take hold, not to expand on a conversation, like I had done previously, but to silence it—to say, "I don't believe," and to see what would happen.

Silence happened, but surprisingly, it was not alienating. It was more like the relief of turning off a constantly dripping tap, or overly loud music. Peace and quiet, uninterrupted by magisterial dictates or philosophical fallacy or wish fulfillment. I recognized in that moment that I had picked the wrong vocation, but I did not know what to do about it.

When you are more than halfway through a Master of Divinity program, you do not have a lot of options. Even though I knew then that I had made the wrong decision choosing theology and chaplaincy as an educational and career path, respectively, I vacillated between walking away without completing my degree and finishing what I had started.

I had already completed most of the course work and spent hundreds of hours working in the outreach program, but the idea of completing another class felt like torture. I was conflicted. I didn't like the idea of not finishing, of what it would say about me to others and to myself. Despite this, I knew I could not tolerate completing my last three courses. Before the next semester started, I booked an appointment with the registrar to talk about my options. The door to her office was ajar. I was afraid when I stepped across the threshold, but her warm smile encouraged me to continue moving forward and to share my dilemma.

Having made the choice to attend a small college, I was on a first-name basis with her. She invited me in to her cozy office, filled with placards and photographs of her many years with the college. On her desk was a picture of her family, her husband and two sons. She encouraged me to have a seat, and I instinctively closed the door behind me and pulled up a chair. When she asked me what brought me in, without thinking, I blurted out, "I don't want to finish my M.Div. I don't believe anymore. What are my options?" Though she seemed somewhat shocked by my impromptu declaration, she did not make a big deal about it. Perhaps this was not the first time she had had this conversation with a student. Without missing a beat, she told me I could leave the program, or I could transfer to the theological studies program, for which I needed only to complete one of my three remaining Old Testament requirements.

I walked out of her office in a haze, confident that I had made a good compromise. I went home, withdrew my applications to the Catholic School Board and the local Catholic Hospital, and waited for the year to hurry up and be over. I did not know what I would do once I graduated; I just knew that the end was near and that, once on the other side, I would have my degree and move on.

I did not have many ideas about how I was going to make a living; I just knew that it would be outside of the Church and that I was not going to go back. Unlike other members of the Clergy Project, I was lucky that I did not then have a family to support as I made the transition to a secular career path. Though I was isolated and fearful of people asking questions about my education, I knew that I could move past it and, at some point, this whole struggle would become a distant memory. Though I felt sad that I had lost my peers and no longer had a spiritual home, I did not allow myself to linger on these emotions, despite the fact that I felt very alone and isolated.

When I turned away from a career in chaplaincy, I did so with little fanfare or explanation. It was as if one day I was counted among believers, doing God's work, and the next, I was not. That day finally came in November 2004, when I received my degree. The transition had its bumps, though thankfully far fewer in number and smaller in size than those experienced by many other members of the Clergy Project. Having left a career with clear job prospects and good job security, I, like so many others, was thrust into an unstable labor market. In my case, I was lucky, as it was less obvious to potential employers that I was transitioning from one career path to another. The problem, however, remained: how would I translate my skills and education in ministry into another field and build my experience and contacts so that I could make the leap into a new career outside of ministry?

Straddled with debt and limited career options, I decided I would parlay my writing and communication skills into a career in public relations and communications. With limited contacts and resources, I signed up for a job search program at a women's center. The first thing that I was told to do was to build a network. In an effort to check this step off my to-do list, I volunteered for the IdeaCity Conference in the summer of 2005. This conference, the brainchild of Canadian media mogul Moses Znaimer, featured speakers from a variety of cultural, scientific, and social backgrounds, each contributing ideas to a converging narrative over a three-day event.

The event was held on the University of Toronto campus, in the Isabel Bader Theatre, located a short distance from where my convocation had taken place just seven months prior. The theatre, a modern steel, stone, and glass structure, stood seamlessly alongside traditionally collegiate architecture, a beautiful juxtaposition of old and new. Inside, the entry and foyer were flooded by light beaming through the two-story tall windows. When I arrived on the first day, staff, other volunteers, and conference attendees milled about. Though I was not a registered attendee, I had received approval to sit in on that morning's second presentation.

All of the five hundred seats in the theatre were filled by the time I entered the theatre. From the back of the house, I saw some standing room near the stage on the right aisle near the wall. I quickly made my way there in time to hear a brief introduction, after which Sam Harris took to the stage to discuss his then new book, *The End of Faith*.

He was dressed casually, in a rather unassuming manner, wearing jeans and a black short-sleeve oxford. I guess I had expected something more "academic" for someone whose book was rattling the bones of organized religion and Western liberal relativism. In a very straightforward and unobtrusive manner, he laid out his core thesis for the audience.

Despite the limited allotted time of twenty minutes, he succinctly and calmly detailed his concerns regarding the "balkanization" of dialogue about religion. In fact, he described his presentation as an attempt to "worry out loud." The audience appeared to appreciate his fortitude and forthrightness, many nodding their heads in agreement. As I stood listening to his comments, I was keen to observe his method of articulating his ideas. Up to that point, I had told very few people that I was an atheist and, indeed, that studying theology had contributed to my disbelief. I was wary of how people might react to this unexpected utterance and, to be honest, felt isolated as a former student of theology who had somehow opened a Pandora's box in her mind and was unable to keep a lid on it. Looking back now, I can see how my Catholic guilt played a role in my self-inflicted censorship.

The session wrapped and the conference attendees, speakers, and staff spilled out into the foyer on their way to lunch. I, along with several other people, stayed back to speak with Sam. I approached him to say how much I had enjoyed his presentation, to which he gave a polite, noncommittal reply, "Thank you very much." A little nervous with the subject matter, I practically blurted out, "I've just graduated with my master's from a theological college on this campus." He appeared a bit surprised, given my praise of his presentation, and seemed to be expecting me to confront him about his arguments. Instead, I leaned forward and practically whispered, "But I'm an atheist." His eyes widened with surprise, and he smiled and asked, "How did that happen?" I rather clumsily detailed my story, elated to have a chance to finally say out loud and without fear of repercussion that I was no longer a believer.

For many years after leaving the church, I lived without community. I was hopelessly unaware that atheists organized and had little to no knowledge of secular humanism. Though I was content with my assertion that religion was a paternalistic fallacy, I thought that my only option was to live without a community based on a common worldview. It was only after my son was born in 2009 that a Google search brought me to the book *Parenting Beyond Belief*, edited by Dale McGowan. Chapter nine in particular jumped out at me, "Seeking Community." I liked the idea of connecting with others who shared my values, specifically, human rights, social justice, and environmentalism. But I was at a loss when it came to finding a group that resonated with me. In many ways, you could say that religion had poisoned my trust in community. I had witnessed first-hand the dysfunctional inner workings of the Church. While working for my diocese, for example, I was paid less and respected less than my male counterparts, even though I operated a pastoral program that did outreach to marginalized communities and brought in revenue via a contract for service with the federal government.

Given such experiences, it is not hard to understand why my satisfaction with the Church eroded and why I was cautious of joining another community. I had seen up close how the institutionalization or branding of morality clutters ethical thinking and warps it into a form of protectionist propaganda. I thought, if the Church could claim moral fortitude yet be utterly ineffectual at implementing and maintaining ethical standards even after nearly two thousand years of experience, how could a bunch of nonbelievers in a newly formed "meet up" plausibly make a claim to moral superiority?

Such doubts and conflict dissuaded me from joining a local humanist group. I vacillated between seeing the potential benefits and being uncertain about putting myself out there. I was also deeply concerned that I would not fit in with a group of atheists. Funny as that now sounds, at the time, I thought atheists would be perplexed and perhaps hostile to the fact that I was a former believer and chaplain. I had no evidence to support this notion, of course, other than my own prejudices that I continued to carry with me after years of deep involvement in the Church. I was prepared for interest in and questions about my loss of faith, but I thought that I might be judged as well, and I was not sure I was ready for that.

Eventually my curiosity and desire for community got the better of me, and I attended my first humanist meet up on a Sunday afternoon in January 2011. The group met at a local community college. I did not know anyone attending the event and quietly introduced myself to an older man with a kindly face who was greeting people at the entrance of the designated classroom. He welcomed me to take a seat at the front, but, feeling a little exposed, I instead took a seat near the back. The room was disorganized, with desks and chairs set up haphazardly in five rows. A group of people busily set up a computer and some AV equipment at the front near the white board. Like the room, the organizers seemed disorganized, but it did not seem to bother them or the others waiting patiently. The informality and lack of rigid structure had an unexpected calming and reassuring effect. I thought to myself, "This is nothing like church. Maybe it will be okay ..."

After a long delay, the organizers began asking people to take their seats. A member of the group then got up and introduced the subject. She was a tall woman with a British accent. In her brief comments, she told us that she had attended the recent Atheist Alliance International/Humanist Canada Convention in Montreal and that she was happy to be able to present a video from the event that she thought the group might find interesting.

The lights dimmed. The projector screen at the front of the room filled with the image of a hotel ballroom, where a group of people gathered around tables to listen to a presentation by a Tufts University philosophy professor whose name I did not then know, Daniel C. Dennett. The title of his talk was, "What Should Replace Religions?" I listened with great interest to his presentation and to his argument that it is the job of humanism to organize a replacement for religion. His comments resonated with me, as someone who had known and experienced the benefits of religious communities, but I was unsure how religion would or could be replaced. I sat deep in thought, pondering his words, when at about the five-minute mark he said something, in a rather understated way, that shocked me, completely interrupting my train of thought: "Last year in Burbank I . . . talked about the confidential survey of closeted nonbelieving preachers."

In a moment, things began to slow down. It was as if everything and every person in the room paused as Dennett's words resonated inside my head. Had I really heard him say that? Did he also just say the findings had been published? The rest of his presentation became like background noise as I began to consider the impact of his statement. If someone was studying this phenomenon, then there were others, hundreds, if not thousands, similar to me. I was dumbfounded and elated in one moment.

It was all I could do to remain in my seat and wait out the meeting. Before making a mad dash out the door, I noticed that someone had printed up copies of the study, published by the journal *Evolutionary Psychology* in March 2010, for those in attendance. I made note of the strikingly matter-of-fact title, "Preachers Who Are Not Believers," and saw that Dennett had written it with Linda LaScola, a qualitative researcher. I grabbed one off the table and headed to my car to read it. I don't think I had ever been so nervous or excited to read something in my entire life. The first few lines of the study's abstract read:

There are systemic features of contemporary Christianity that create an almost invisible class of non-believing clergy, ensnared in their ministries by a web of obligations, constraints, comforts, and community. Exemplars from five Protestant denominations, Southern Baptist, United Church of Christ, Presbyterian, Methodist, and Church of Christ, were found and confidentially interviewed at length about their lives, religious education and indoctrination, aspirations, problems and ways of coping. The in-depth, qualitative interviews formed the basis for profiles of all five, together with general observations about their predicaments and how they got into them.

Here in black and white I had proof that I was not the only one! I called my husband to tell him. All I could say was, "I am not the only one, I am not the only one."

2

MAKING THINGS HAPPEN

*"From whom the whole body, joined and knit together by every
ligament with which it is equipped, as each part is working properly,
promotes the body's growth in building itself up in love."*
—Ephesians 4:16

I see now how the years following my leaving the Church
and ministry were ones of self-imposed isolation. I felt
different from my classmates at seminary. Despite the relief
of personally acknowledging my disbelief, I felt the shame
of difference. It was not an alien experience to feel that
way given that I had been a woman in a Roman Catholic
seminary. And so, I had retreated away from community and
accepted an exiled purgatory. Up to that point, I had thought
of myself as some sort of anomaly, a rare blip on a screen. But
the study by Dennett and LaScola provided evidence that I
was not. As soon as I returned home that afternoon from my
first humanist gathering, I e-mailed Dennett.

To: Dennett, Daniel C.
Subject: study - ministers who are closeted atheists
Sent: Sunday, January 23, 2011 4:43 PM

Dear Dr. Dennett:
A member of my local humanist group attended the AAI-HC Conference in Montreal and she, a retired therapist, told me about your research.
I have a master in theology and I determined during the course of my studies that I do not believe in god.
I would be interested in taking part in your study, if you are still looking for candidates.
Sincerely,
Catherine

To: Catherine Dunphy
Subject: Re: study - ministers who are closeted atheists
Sent: Sunday, January 23, 2011 5:25 PM

I have sent your email to Linda LaScola. Thanks for expressing your interest in participating. We will put your name and address in our files.
DCD

To: Catherine Dunphy
Subject: Re: study - ministers who are closeted atheists
Sent: Sunday, January 23, 2011 6:44 PM

Thanks for contacting Dan Dennett about our study. He forwarded your email to me, because I am conducting the interviews.
Our schedule for Phase II of the study is a bit up in the air right now, but we were thinking about including people who studied theology but did not become clergy.
Could you tell me a little about yourself and your experience? What was your religious denomination? What school of theology did you attend? What was your purpose? (E.g., to become ordained clergy? to teach?)
Thanks,
Linda LaScola

In the span of a few hours, I had gone from being in utter isolation to having the simple knowledge that there were others like me out there. I still had no way to connect with these newly discovered peers, but knowing that they existed was in many ways comforting.

Becoming a member of the Clergy Project was not something that was even on my radar when I first began communicating with Linda about their study—after all, the Clergy Project did not yet exist. In our first conversations, she was considerate but cautious, asking me questions about my background, such as how and why I came to be a nonreligious Roman Catholic woman trained to be a chaplain. I was so happy to be speaking with someone who had met others like me, that I eagerly answered all of Linda's questions, providing what I am sure was an overabundance of information. I also specifically asked whether it would be possible to be put in touch with other study participants. Linda said confidentiality restrictions made that impossible, but she did indicate that others like me were out there who would also like an opportunity to meet. Without naming names, she then revealed that a group of supporters was trying to create a safe place online where we could connect.

When I left my faith behind, I never would have imagined an online forum made specifically to facilitate peer interaction and support for nonbelieving clergy, as I thought that my journey to atheism was rare. After I left the Church, my life for a time became a series of contradictions. I was overjoyed to be unburdened by my previous faith, but still struggled with the loss of community and isolation. So, when I discovered the existence of other nonbelieving clergy after viewing Daniel

Dennett's presentation and reading his study with Linda LaScola, my immediate response was, "I have to know them." It was like peeking through a crack in a door that had long been closed off. All I wanted to do was to tear down the door and connect with others who had followed a similar path.

Religious nonbelievers may not have faith in the efficacy of prayer, but in many ways, the "safe place" to which Linda had referred—the yet unnamed Clergy Project—served as an answer to my unarticulated prayer. In March 2011, I, along with fifty-one other former and active nonbelieving clergy, was given the opportunity to join the forum at its launch. Most of the members remained closeted and had not come out to the world or to their communities about their atheism. Many of us were both excited and terrified, yet inside the virtual world of the Web, a hidden space had been carved out for us to speak our secrets freely.

The seeds for this space, I would soon learn, had been sown in a series of conversations between Richard Dawkins, the famed evolutionary biologist, and Dan Barker, copresident of the Freedom From Religion Foundation, about the plight of clergy who no longer believed in god. Richard and Dan both recognized the quandary of nonbelieving clergy—specifically, that they were isolated and that, given their dependency on religion with regard to their employment, communities, and family, they were in need of assistance. These conversations, coupled with the great interest that had met the Dennett and LaScola study, led to a January 2011 meeting between Linda LaScola, Dan Barker, and Robin Elisabeth Cornwell, then the executive director of the Richard Dawkins Foundation for Reason and Science, at the Mitsitam Café in the National Museum of the American Indian in Washington, DC. During this meeting, which occurred only a couple weeks before I first began communicating with Linda, they laid the plans for the Clergy Project. Two still-closeted active clergy, "Adam" and "Chris," worked in tandem with these secular leaders to set up and monitor the private Clergy Project forum, with additional support and assistance from the staff at the Richard Dawkins Foundation for Reason and Science.

Despite being one of the original fifty-two original members of the Clergy Project, I could do little more than wait in the wings as the forum was being built, and I had no detailed knowledge about how the project came to be or what direction it would take. Only in preparation for this book have I come to appreciate how quickly and effectively these "supporters," as Linda had referred to them in our early communications, worked to make the Clergy Project a reality. Rather than filter their recollections only through my own subjective lens, I will share with you here their exact words regarding the formation and creation of the project, as well as their motivations for creating it and for providing support to wayward religious leaders.

Richard Dawkins

There are many converging opinions about Richard Dawkins. Some people adore him as an atheist "rock star," while others vilify him as an angry atheist. These characterizations are both a pale shadow of the person and the lightning rod that is Richard Dawkins. I would say that he is first and foremost a humanist—a caring, charitable person who strives to support human well-being. He does not play to vanities, but challenges his friends and foes alike to be reasoned, deliberate, and compassionate. He acknowledges the potential impact that the Clergy Project could have, envisioning a future where the power of religious indoctrination and superstition is overtaken by reason and compassion.

With this spirit—and with the support of his foundation, which continues to provide operational assistance to the project—he was not only instrumental in the Clergy Project's founding but also in ensuring its continued growth.

Who were your first conversations with, regarding the existence of nonbelieving clergy?
Dan Barker and I had a first conversation about this, I think, in Australia at a conference.

What was your motivation for helping to found and support the group of atheist clergy that we now know as the Clergy Project?
For me it goes back a long way. My most ambitious scheme never really came to fruition. I tried to think when setting up my foundation, really talking with Robin Cornwell; we discussed what we would do if we had a lot of money, what would we do. One of the things we thought of was a grant for ex-clergypeople, to rescue them, as we recognized that a clergyperson who lost their faith was vulnerable to not just social pressure but also financial. So, we were thinking of scholarships to retrain, maybe for a year, and I think we were thinking in rather ambitious terms. What we should have done actually would be instead of thinking in terms of giving scholarships to lots of people, just picking one or two as a publicity stunt really, but we thought that would not be possible.

I have known Dan Dennett for years and I was interested in his point of view of the research that he and Linda LaScola were doing. Then I started talking to other people who had had a similar idea, like Todd Stiefel [note: founder and president of the Stiefel Freethought Foundation]. I realized that it could be something much more modest and that is what the Clergy Project turned out to be, and it ended up that my foundation supported the infrastructure for the Web site, rather than actually giving grants. Then we stood back and let the members of the project run it themselves.

You have been very generous in making your foundation and its staff available to support and sustain the Clergy Project. It is not something that is well known.
Well, I think Robin Cornwell deserves a lot of credit for that. She is the unsung hero behind the scenes.

Is there anything you would like the secular movement as a whole or the Clergy Project to accomplish?
Well, I would like to see a mass migration of clergy out of religion, not just in America but also in Ireland. I think that the Catholic Church is worried; they are hardly getting any new priests.

Though I do want to see the Catholic Church die, on the other hand, I think Islam is such a fantastic evil in the world, and in a way, especially in Africa, I could imagine seeing Christianity as a pull against Islam. I remember that phrase, "Always keep a hold of nurse, for fear of finding something worse."

What influence do you think or hope the Clergy Project will have?
I had not thought about it, so I am not arguing from authority, but I think the best influence would be on other clergy people, to show them the way. That can help give them courage.

Dan Barker
As copresident of the Freedom From Religion Foundation (FFRF), along with his wife, Annie Laurie Gaylor, Dan Barker

is a well-known spokesperson for the secular movement. He has spent nearly thirty years working to cement the barrier between church and state. Given his history as a former evangelical minister, Dan is not just a founder of the Clergy Project but also a member, making him the only secular founder with direct access to the private forum. In his book *Godless: How an Evangelical Preacher Became one of America's Leading Atheists*, Dan details his deconversion story. His years of experience "on the outside" are a continued source of encouragement for members of the project still in ministry, and he continues to reach out to members in need of secular "pastoral" care. In addition, Dan and Annie Laurie have both supported the Clergy Project by offering the assistance of the Freedom From Religion Foundation.

Did you at any time think something might come from your early conversations with Richard Dawkins about nonbelieving clergy—for example, whether it would spawn a community or a movement?

No, I did not think it would be a movement. Richard and I just thought it would be a project to help some clergy in need. We did not envision the forum or community at that time. In fact, when we talked during dinner in Copenhagen—which was the second time we had brought up the subject, I think the first time was in Iceland—Richard at first said that we could probably raise some money to help a few clergy, but that it probably wouldn't become a big thing. We could do it for a while, and then use that fact to advertise the problem. Neither of us thought it through beyond that point.

What was your experience like when you left ministry in the 1980s? Did you feel adrift like many members do now?

I actually didn't feel adrift. I immediately got in touch with other freethinkers, through FFRF, and gradually came into contact with other former clergy.

What do you hope the Clergy Project will achieve?
We want to help people in the real world who are suffering. We also want to point out that even among the most educated and devoted followers of a religion, there are legitimate doubts. If the clergy themselves don't believe it, then why should anyone else?

What do you think will be the project's impact on organized religion?
Organized religion is already diminishing on its own. The Clergy Project will only hasten its demise.

Daniel C. Dennett
A professor of philosophy at Tufts University who first made a name for himself with his work on consciousness, free will, and evolution, Daniel C. Dennett later wrote the best-selling book, *Breaking the Spell: Religion as a Natural Phenomenon*, which calls for the scientific study of religion. This eventually led him to collaborate with Linda LaScola in their study of five Protestant ministers who lacked belief in God. Four of the five would be counted among the initial fifty-two founding members of the Clergy Project. They expanded on their initial study in their book, *Caught in the Pulpit: Leaving Belief Behind.*

Can you tell me about your research with Linda LaScola and its role in helping to bring about the Clergy Project?
Well, Richard Dawkins and I had been talking off and on for years about the prospect of starting something like a halfway house for

nonbelieving clergy, but I didn't have that in mind at all when Linda and I began our collaboration. In retrospect, the Clergy Project was a natural byproduct, but it wasn't something I had expected or hoped for. The confidentiality of our interview process was in fact designed to preserve the anonymity, the insulation in effect, of all our interviewees, so it was a surprise to me when I learned that some of them had nevertheless found each other through Dan Barker. Even before we started the LaScola interviews, I had a pretty good idea that there must be many clergy wishing they had a graceful way out of their predicaments, and when this was confirmed by our interviews, I realized that this was something we could do to help them.

What role do you see the Clergy Project having?

In the short run, it will not only provide guidance and support and community for those who are trapped in their pulpits, but also provide a perspective on the clerical life that might alert many idealistic young people to the dangers, and dissuade them from committing themselves to such a life. This in turn might starve the churches of pastors and priests, until they have to let in the sunlight and change the nature of ministry altogether. Ideally, individual churches or whole denominations might quite forthrightly forsake the double-talk and hypocrisy and make it clear to young and old within the church that these rituals are symbolic celebrations of life, illustrated with strange and wonderful myths that can inspire us to live better lives, and that there is no obligation to try to believe in their literal truth. Then church services could evolve into a new kind of theatre, intended to refocus folks' attention on things more important than their mundane projects, and inspiring them to contribute their time, effort, and yes, money to making the world a better place.

Linda LaScola

Linda LaScola contacted Dennett after reading his work on religion and suggested collaborating on a qualitative research project to examine the phenomenon of clergy who lacked belief in god. This led to their study, "Preachers Who Are Not Believers," and later to their book, *Caught in the Pulpit*. Since the Clergy Project's inception, Linda has willingly offered her expertise in research and social work to the benefit of the project's operations, and she continues to provide ongoing help to the Clergy Project by offering her time as press coordinator.

Did you have any expectations with your initial research?
It never crossed my mind that our research would be related to a new community of nonbelieving clergy. When talking to people about the Clergy Project, I always make a point to say that it wasn't my idea, but I'm so glad Dan Barker and Richard Dawkins thought of it.

When did conversations about setting up a Web site for nonbelieving clergy begin?
The first in-person conversation was a meeting with Robin Cornwell, formerly of the Richard Dawkins Foundation, Dan Barker, and me at the American Indian Museum cafeteria on a Sunday morning in January 2011. The result of that meeting was a commitment of funds and Web support from the Richard Dawkins Foundation and a commitment from Dan Barker and me to contact prospective members to inform them about the incipient private Web site and invite them to join. The private site was "up" in March.

What was your role after launch?
Once the sites were up and running, my behind-the-scenes help has been in responding to press inquiries and in selecting and training

screeners to take over the job of screening potential new members that Dan Barker and I initially did. The screeners, members who are "out" former clergy, were easy to train. They already had their own experience of being nonbelieving clergy, plus they were extremely conscientious about screening people well and welcoming them into the group.

Regarding press inquiries, I had gained experience dealing with the press after our pilot study was published and national and international media contacted Dan Dennett and me about interviewing our participants, while protecting their privacy. Thus, I became a "natural" for the job of press contact. It is one of the few useful jobs that I could legitimately do for the project. It would not be right for a nonmember to do new-member screening. Screening press requests keeps me quite busy at times, as requests come in from all over the world.

Do you have any hopes or aspirations for the Project?

My hope is that the organization grows and thrives and eventually becomes obsolete and morphs into something else. I hope the members can not only support each other, but can help move society from being de facto faith-based to being more openly humanistic. I hope that as times goes on there will be fewer nonbelieving clergy, because fewer people who eventually become nonbelievers will become clergy in the first place. I hope there will be an outlet for the good people I've met during the study and through the Clergy Project that allows them to use their talents and find meaningful work without going through the process of religious indoctrination followed by a slow and difficult shedding of their religious beliefs.

Robin Elisabeth Cornwell

As the former executive director of the Richard Dawkins

Foundation for Reason and Science, Robin Elisabeth Cornwell led the charge in meeting the operational needs of the private Clergy Project members' forum. She immediately began assisting with the construction of the forum, making staff from the foundation available to help "Adam" and "Chris" with its construction. Her efforts paid off and, in less than three months, the forum went from idea to reality.

Can you tell me about how the Clergy Project came about?
On January 9, 2011, Linda LaScola, Dan Barker, and I met at the American Indian Museum in DC to discuss the nascent idea of helping unbelieving clergy. Linda's study had been very in-depth and many of her participants expressed a need to move forward and find a path out of their theological dissonance. Dan Barker, as an ex-preacher, not only understood the problems these men and women were facing, but had contacts with numerous ex-clergy who had given up their belief in the supernatural. The Richard Dawkins Foundation had the talent and dedication to put together a Web site that would allow unbelieving clergy to safely communicate with one another.

What motivated you to be involved?
For my part, I felt a strong desire to offer help to the men and women who were trapped in difficult situations. Not only could these individuals lose their jobs and livelihood, they risked losing their families, friends, and community. I have heard many nonbelievers chastise, even denigrate, individuals who could not tell their spouses or families of their atheism. Their intolerance for those who were not open about their nonbelief was an antithesis of my view of how humans should live with and judge one another. It has been my hope of greater tolerance that was the impetus of the OUT Campaign [note: a campaign she initiated in 2007 to create public awareness of atheists], and the Clergy Project was a natural extension of that

movement. *As a minority, nonbelievers need to reach out to one another and offer support rather than condemn one another for not being cookie-cutter atheists. There is no such thing as a prototypical "atheist," just as there is no such thing as a prototypical Christian, Jew, Muslim, Buddhist, or Hindu. The individuals who have come into the Clergy Project bring with them a diversity from which all of us can learn and grow.*

How did you get the task accomplished so quickly?

It seemed to take forever to get it up and running. We were terribly impatient. The most important aspect of the project was that the members drove it. It did not matter what Linda or I wanted, or for that matter what Richard Dawkins or Dan Dennett wanted. The Web team that worked on this project understood its significance, and all of them said what an honor and privilege it was to build something that could help people. In our day-to-day lives, most of us do not get to do that. The members consisted of nonbelievers still working in the clergy and members who had already "come out" and were living secular lives. The concept was to allow them to safely talk to one another, without any fear of rebuke. We lived by the rule, "Do not judge lest ye be judged."

What I personally found so touching was the sense of humor and commitment the members projected. As the Web site launched, and members started to interact, the team that were not either clergy or ex-clergy left the site. The web designers only interacted on technical problems. Our role was completed, and it was in the hands of the members to make the Clergy Project a success.

Is there something you would like to see the Clergy Project accomplish?

I feel extremely honored to have been part of the Clergy Project, and what I hope for it is that it continues to grow and help those who find themselves in seemingly impossible positions. It would be great if the project could offer more opportunities for men and women trying to leave the clergy to find new careers that optimize their talents, desire to help others, and significant experience.

"Adam"

As a founder and closeted member of the project, "Adam" is one of the heroes of the Clergy Project. His efforts in setting up and monitoring the project, as well as his work on the board of directors, cannot be measured. When I first "met" him through the forum, I learned that he worked as a worship pastor at a church with 500–750 members in the southern United States. I also recognized his pseudonym and story from the Dennett and LaScola study, in which he was one of the five nonbelieving pastors profiled.

What was your motivation for working on this high-profile project?

There was no project in mind when I called FFRF to speak with Dan Barker in 2009. I had been studying on my own for about seven or eight months. It was the day after Easter Sunday services and I knew I had to seek help from someone. My first contact with Linda LaScola was in April of 2009. My ongoing conversations with Linda and Dan Barker grew to include Robin Cornwell and eventually Richard Dawkins. In the meantime, these folks were talking about helping nonbelieving clergy and the idea of a safe place online materialized. I agreed to help as I could and planning began for the creation of the private forum. I guess I was just in the right place at the right time with the right skills and motivation to contribute. In January 2011, I began working with the team from the Richard Dawkins Foundation to build a private forum.

We launched the forum to invitation-only members on March 21, 2011.

Are there any goals that you would like to see the project accomplish?

I would like for the project to first and foremost be a safe place for closeted nonbelieving clergy. A place to find hope and encouragement for those who are courageously choosing, for reasons most cannot understand, to live carefully in two worlds. Most find themselves precariously balancing their inner emotions and character because they care about how their change of beliefs will affect others. Secondly, I want the project to raise awareness of the growing trend toward reason over faith—even in the religious community.

Given your pivotal role in founding the project, is there anything you hope it will accomplish?

I think organized religion will take note of the Clergy Project because it cannot totally be ignored. However, I think they will only be able to look at and interpret it through their clouded and scaled eyes of faith. For the majority it will simply reinforce their belief that good and evil are constantly at war and that this is merely a manifestation of evil overcoming some of the faithful. It may even invigorate them to keep a closer watch on the leaders. That being said, some, a small number, will possibly have the courage to consider and even question organized religion and the concept of god in general. The goal of the Clergy Project is not to deconvert clergy but to assist those who are at that point already.

"Chris"

When the Clergy Project started, Chris was still in active ministry as a senior pastor in an evangelical denomination.

Despite this, he worked diligently to ready the private forum for launch. Chris was one of the first friends that I made on the forum. Listening to his story, and that of other active clergy, motivated me to offer to help with the project.

Tell me about your transition out of faith?
My transition out of a position of supernaturalism began as a long theological examination of my own beliefs. I have never been a fundamentalist, or even a conservative, but I did hold a supernaturalist position until about 2008. I had long since jettisoned the idea of a literal hell, partly because the Bible does not support such an idea and partly due to a struggle to understand theodicy. That led to a position of universalism, which ironically is well supported in the Bible. However, I also began around this time to examine miracle claims from a skeptical viewpoint. This in turn led to a general application of skeptical principles to all supernaturalist claims. In time, by around late 2010, I had come to a fully naturalist position. I still believed in many of the moral teachings of Jesus (those that could be legitimately attributed to him), but no longer believed him to be unique or divine. My major influences during this period were the writings of Victor Stenger, Bart Ehrman, and Dan Barker, as well as numerous podcasts.

How did you first become involved with the Clergy Project?
I became involved with the Clergy Project when I contacted Dan Barker, who I knew had also been in the ministry. I wrote to ask his advice for transition out of the ministry, and discovered that he had been compiling an anonymous list of pastors like me for some time. He told me about his desire to create a more developed network of pastors who were trying to leave the ministry, and connected me with another pastor, "Adam," with whom he had been discussing the topic. "Adam" and I then became involved in the initial planning stages with Dan and others, as well as becoming the eventual moderators of

the site. I am proud to say that I am the second clergy member of the Clergy Project.

What has the project meant to you and what impact do you think it might have on organized religion?
The Clergy Project primarily offers a way to connect with other like-minded pastors who are struggling over the same issues. While we might not have all the answers, we do have listening ears and common experiences. For this reason, I believe the Clergy Project means hope, in a very real sense. I think that the vast majority of leaders of organized religion will continue to have an antagonistic position toward the Clergy Project. Fundamentalists and evangelicals will see us as hopeless apostates, liberals will see us as burnouts, and will wonder why we cannot just continue to obfuscate our language as they do, and progressives will see us as competition for the post-religious community. However, a growing number of laypersons will see us as the brave ones, the true prophets, the ones who are willing to stand up and say that we can no longer bear the standard of supernaturalism. This will give them a new boldness to do the same, and within a decade or two organized religion will be past the point of recovery. In North America, it will become a quaint but irrelevant relic of a bygone era, as it has in Europe. While this is the inevitable outcome of today's emerging paradigm, and will happen regardless of the Clergy Project, our impact on the religious community will only serve to speed the demise of organized religion's influence in our culture.

What was it like when you first became involved with the project, and what do you hope it will accomplish in the future?
I cannot describe the relief and joy I felt simply to learn that I was not alone. I was not the only pastor who was moving out of supernaturalism, and I was not crazy. My motivation for committing

my time and effort to the Clergy Project was based in the knowledge that many others needed to experience that same relief, and to find the connections to others that I had found. It was a truly thrilling experience to be helping to develop a hidden network of people who could literally be the salvation for one another. From the beginning, my hope was that the Clergy Project would become a seedbed for an organized alternative to supernaturalism and religion. Its members possess a vast wealth of knowledge concerning many issues that face the human condition, are experienced in developing and leading grassroots organizations, and understand the importance of symbol, myth, and narrative to many people. For this reason, they are perfectly poised to be the vanguard of a new social movement that would offer humanistic, naturalistic community to the world. While other organizations offer this, they are not generally influenced by the unique experience of former clergy.

Did you have any concerns about the direction of the project?
My greatest fear from the beginning was that the Clergy Project would be subsumed into the atheist movement. Many Clergy Project members, myself included, will never self-identify as atheists because it's a negative position. It describes only what one does not believe, rather than the beliefs and values that one does hold. I find it much healthier and accurate to describe myself as a post-supernaturalistic humanist, as do many Clergy Project members. And contrary to the claims of many in the atheist movement, spirituality does not necessarily imply supernaturalism. Sadly, the leaders of the atheist movement often have a deeply flawed view of religion and the religious community, and lack a real understanding of religious perspectives. They would do well to learn from the experiences and knowledge of Clergy Project members, but I have encountered a profound unwillingness on their part to do so. I believe the position I hold also mirrors the position of the many thousands of laypersons who are leaving religion. They

still want community, social outreach, shared values, narrative, symbol, and even myth to be a valuable part of their lives. And most Clergy Project members still have a real need to lead communities in these areas. I believe that an organized approach to providing for these needs from a naturalistic perspective will be the greatest gift the Clergy Project can give the world. As more and more people leave organized religion, the Clergy Project stands poised to provide an organized community for this emerging social movement.

3

GOING LIVE

"Wandering from nation to nation,
from one kingdom to another people."
—Psalm 105:13

In the few months that I waited for the Clergy Project to transform from an idea into reality, I had plenty of time to think over the implications of how much I had missed having friends and peers with whom I could relate. When I left the Church, I limped away. Looking back on it now, I can see that I underwent a type of grieving—one that could be likened to what you might experience following a divorce or the ending of an unhappy relationship. Once I was out of the Church and secured employment elsewhere, I had a great sense of relief. Although I was not then open with many people about my journey to atheism, I was overjoyed to be outside of the influence of the Church. It felt like I had escaped the demands of an overbearing parent, that I was free to make my own choices, and that no one, aside from myself, was keeping score. To this day, I am still grateful that I am no longer inside the Church or struggling to be a believer. But that does not mean that there were not positive things that I had to forfeit to gain my freedom.

During the years between my acceptance of my atheism and my participation as a member of the Clergy Project, I wallowed in a type of self-imposed isolation. I intentionally lived in the closet. Retreating from habits and hobbies that had previously brought contentment into my life, I consigned myself to the naive belief that there were not others like me out there in the world. And if there were, there would be no hope of knowing them. I felt different and was different from my friends who grew up marginally religious and for whom faith had always had little relevance. I felt uncomfortable talking about my previous beliefs and attempted to avoid conversations related to religion at all costs.

I recognized that I was very angry with the Church—not only for the indoctrination that I had experienced and the stack of falsehoods it had forced me to choke down, but also for the years that I had spent sacrificing my own happiness so that I could be of service to its mandate. This experience has not been unlike being very angry with a parent or mentor after you discover their major faults. When it comes to the Church, you don't have to look hard to see its refusal to acknowledge its deficits, which are exhibited in its continued devotion to the magisterium and its run-amok theocratic egotism. The Church relentlessly demands capitulation from believers and nonbelievers alike.

I know that I do not paint a very pretty picture of the Church, and this is despite the fact that there are things about my previous faith that I miss, and even mourn. But the simple reality for me is that the ideas and beliefs that the Church espouses and propagates, in its long-established statements of faith, are much less important than the universal values of compassion, love, and community. Though the Church may attempt to brand these as its values, it continually fails by requiring its followers to forfeit their conscience to the demands and confines of faith. The Church sees itself as the world's primary human institution, which might explain why it reacts as it does when someone questions its authority or does not follow in the direction it leads.

Although these sentiments had occupied my thoughts since I had left the Church, I never thought I would find others of like mind with a similar set of personal experiences. As a result, those few weeks after I first contacted Daniel Dennett and Linda LaScola were an exciting time. Though I had not yet spoken to another nonbelieving active or former clergyperson, I knew that I was not alone, and that simple knowledge meant a lot to me. Though Linda did not share details regarding the other members, she did share the news that we would soon have a safe place to meet and an opportunity to get to know one another and perhaps even form a community. I only found out the name of the project just before I received my invitation to join the private members-only forum. I am told the planning group went through several naming attempts before settling on the Clergy Project.

Finally, on March 23, 2011, I received the e-mail I had been eagerly anticipating:

Dear Catherine,
You are invited!
The Clergy Project is ready to open! Please follow link provided below and log on to the site, and be sure to go directly to the "Welcome" page where Richard, Dan Barker, Dan Dennett, Linda, Adam, and Chris are there to greet you.

I remember the day very clearly. Excited and nervous, I sat at my kitchen table with my laptop, the sunlight streaming in from the window, as I read the message. Outside the world was warming up for spring, and I was only too happy to stay indoors, stare at my computer, and join the virtual community that I had just been invited to as a member. I immediately logged into the private forum and was ecstatic to read the following welcome messages:

Welcome from Richard Dawkins
Welcome to the Clergy Project. It is hard to think of any other profession, which it is so near to, impossible to leave. If a farmer tires of the outdoor life and wants to become an accountant or a teacher or a shopkeeper, he faces difficulties, to be sure. He must learn new skills, raise money, and move to another area perhaps. But he does not risk losing all his friends, being cast out by his family, being ostracized by his whole community. Clergy who lose their faith suffer double jeopardy. It is as though they lose their job and their marriage and their children on the same day. It is an aspect of the vicious intolerance of religion that a mere change of mind can redound so cruelly on those honest enough to acknowledge it.

The Clergy Project exists to provide a safe haven, a forum where clergy who have lost their faith can meet each other, exchange views, swap problems, counsel each other—for, whatever they may have lost, clergy know how to counsel and comfort. Here you will find confidentiality, sympathy, and a friendly place where you can take your time before deciding how to extricate yourself and when you will feel yourself to stand up and face the cool, refreshing wind of truth.
- Richard Dawkins

Welcome from Dan Dennett
Bon Voyage!
I want to congratulate all those who worked so hard to make The Clergy Project a reality, and to let you all know how proud I am to have played a role in its inception. I can't call this a Welcome message since I am neither host nor guest. But I am very happy to witness the launching of this vessel, and to offer my wishes to all who are getting on board for a safe journey to better places.
-Dan Dennet

Welcome from Dan Barker

I wish there had been a place like this back in the summer of 1983, when after 19 years of evangelical preaching I realized I had gradually grown into an atheist. I still preached for four or five months after that until I decided, "enough is enough." I have told my story in the book, *Godless: How An Evangelical Preacher Became One of America's Leading Atheists* (Foreword by Richard Dawkins), and since that time I have heard from many others in a similar predicament, as well as many who have successfully made the happy transition to "civilian life."

As far as I know, the origin of The Clergy Project has three sources. First, I have been collecting stories of former clergy for more than two decades, but have not yet done anything with them. (Perhaps they will end up in a book—or at least on this site. Many of those people are joining us here, which is very exciting!) At least fifteen years ago Levi Fragell, a former fundamentalist pastor who has since been involved with the Norwegian Humanists, suggested to me that we should form a society of "fallen preachers" (ha), but nothing ever came of that suggestion. (He has been bugging me about it for years.) The February 2008 issue of *Psychology Today* included the story "When Faith Fails: An Atheist in the Pulpit," by Bruce Grierson, which included me and a number of other former and current ministers who have "seen the light," and I am still hearing from preachers as a result of that article.

Second, philosopher Daniel Dennett and researcher Linda LaScola did a preliminary study of "Preachers Who Are Not Believers," which was published in March 2010. A couple of the clergy in that study were ministers in the pulpit who had contacted me after learning of my story, and I was able to suggest them to Dan and Linda. One or two of them (as far as I know) are currently here on this site, still preaching, wanting to get out. This project would not have come together without the input and hard work of Dan and Linda, as well as the active clergy with whom they have built relationships. Since neither Dan nor Linda is a current or former clergy, they will not be participating directly in this site, but we can't ignore their work.

The third origin, the main impetus for the existence of the site itself, is the most important in practical terms. In 2006, just before *The God Delusion* came out, I met Richard Dawkins at the Humanist conference in Reykjavik, Iceland, where he heard me tell my preacher-to-atheist story. He expressed an interest in helping clergy. About three years ago, when Richard wrote the Foreword to my book *Godless*, he again mentioned casually to me that we might want to do something to help clergy get out of the ministry. (I am sure he has been saying this to others as well.) Last summer (June, 2010), when we met for the "Gods and Politics" Atheism Conference in Copenhagen, Richard brought it up again. But how to find those clergy?

The answer is this preliminary attempt to form a free, friendly gathering place for those of us who have changed our beliefs. Eventually, we hope the word will get out and other de-converting clergy will be attracted to join in. Robin Cornwell of the RDFRS, a tireless and creative organizer, has been primarily responsible for the nuts-and-bolts of getting the project off the ground. Without her hard work (and investment by RDFRS), none of this would have happened.

So welcome to something truly historical: the first association of active and former clergy who are now nonbelievers. Freethought is a movement with no followers: we are all leaders, and what happens from here is up to you. If you are currently an "active" minister or priest, then you might benefit from meeting people in similar situations and knowing how others of us have successfully made it out. If you are an "alumnus" or "veteran" clergy, then you certainly have a lot to offer!

-Dan Barker

Welcome from Linda LaScola
Hello, I'm so happy you're here. Having spoken to many of you, I'm eager for you to have the chance to get to know each other. I'll be here for a few days while you're settling in, and then I'll sign off so you can talk among yourselves. I'll be in touch with some of you to participate in the on-going Dennett-LaScola study. Meanwhile, best wishes to all of you and to this unique new community.

-Linda LaScola

Welcome from Adam & Chris
Wow! We finally have a place for free-thought clergy to find refuge, reason, encouragement, and community. I'm really looking forward to meeting everyone, or at least getting to know you by your anonymous names. First, let me say that safety is the top priority on this site. Believe me, I know how important it is that your identity be kept confidential. I don't want to know your real name and I am not going to tell you mine. At least not until we get out of ministry and are ready to do so. So, until then, let's get to know one another, share our journeys, bounce ideas off

each other, and learn from those who have gone before us, the "alumni." So explore the site, make new friends and contribute. This is your site!

- Adam & Chris

I poured over their words, awed and grateful that these people had come together to make this community happen. I then set up my profile, picked an avatar, and began to read the profiles of the other fifty-one members. I noticed that I already had two messages in my inbox, one from Adam and the other from Chris, welcoming me to this safe little community:

Hi, I am Adam. I am a worship pastor at a church of 500-750 members in the southern United States. I have been in ministry for just over 25 years. I was one of the five non-believing pastors in the first Dan Dennett/Linda LaScola study, and one of the team of members to put together this site.

I am technically a free-thought agnostic humanist, but for all practical purposes, I suppose one could just call me an atheist when it comes to the god(s) of scripture.

I have a conservative fundamental Christian wife, but my son and daughter know my secret and why I want to leave the ministry.

Hey! I'm Chris, one of the volunteer moderators/administrators of this site. I'm currently serving as a Senior Pastor in an evangelical denomination, but I'm actively working to find a way out of the ministry.

Over the past few years, through many hours of study, I have come to the conclusion that no theistic claims have any real merit. Through a deep and intense study of the Bible, I now see it as a disjointed compilation of often immoral and conflicting teachings. Now, I have a thoroughly naturalistic worldview.

While labels can often fall short, I consider myself to be a secular humanist (or rational post-theist, or naturalistic humanist, or . . .)

I am fortunate in that my wife shares my views, and we have come to our current positions together. We are raising our young son to be a freethinker, questioning everything and testing all claims.

My hope is that through this forum, new networks and relationships will develop that will build a movement of formerly religious leaders who will pave the way for a new way of being human.

I replied to Adam and Chris, thanking them, expressing my excitement and anticipation for this community. These early interactions amazed me. For so many years after completing my degree, I felt like I was somehow "defective," that something had to have happened to me, as I had to be the only person who went through seminary and came out an atheist. "Adam," "Chris," "Dennis," "Jerry," "Mary," and the others, whom I only knew through pseudonyms, changed that opinion. It had been determined early on that protecting the anonymity and privacy of the members of this new group was of utmost concern, given the potential for harm if members' true identifies and beliefs were exposed publicly. That was why each of the new members invited to join had been thoroughly screened, a process that continues to this day for all new members.

The two initial screeners for the project, Dan Barker and Linda LaScola, agreed to what now have become the standard eligibility criteria for membership in the Clergy Project. First, potential members must have graduated from seminary or have been certified by their religious tradition or denomination as clergy, and be an active or former religious leader or educator of clergy in a seminary or theological school. Second, prospective members must have made the transition from belief in supernaturalism to unbelief. Third and finally, the applicant must now identify as a nonbeliever, post-theist, atheist, agnostic, nontheistic, or freethinker.

My new community grew to include friends from all around the world who, like me, had encountered the pain and isolation of losing their faith. We may be seen by some believers as individuals who have lost our way—but once people take the time to talk to us, to listen, their opinions change. Indeed, in many instances it was a desire to serve better and to help more that led us down the road of doubt and to the Clergy Project. When it comes down to it, though our personal beliefs in an intangible, unsubstantiated all-powerful deity may have changed, very little else about us has been altered. This desire to help others did not fade with our faith, and remains one of the most striking similarities that the members of the Clergy Project share. Given how closely clergy work with their communities, we see rather glaringly that people are not in need of faith; they are in need of personal relationships. We are communal animals. We succeed and fail by the measure of how well we can work together. Humanity's accomplishments in art, architecture, science, and even politics can each be attributed to our ability to collaborate, to listen, and to work in tandem toward a common goal.

The first few weeks after the birth of the Clergy Project witnessed a flurry of online activity. Many stories were shared on the forum and with this, friendships were forged. I don't think that I was alone in my surprise at how many similarities I found among members of the project, despite the fact that we often came from different faith traditions and from different corners of the world. Aside from our desire to do good, Clergy Project members also tend to be musically inclined, active volunteers in their communities, and, for those who have left ministry, involved in helping professions, such as social work, nonprofit service, counseling, and psychotherapy.

Some might expect former religious leaders to have had had their fill of articulating the awe in life. I have found, however, that this is not the case. Although project members no longer will themselves to see an invisible supernatural hand moving throughout the course of human history, they do not see life as a story of the mundane. Rather, they see life as an awe-inspiring challenge. In this newfound awareness, we can not only see the true nature of our universe and the cosmic events that got this billions-of-years-long journey on a roll, but we can also learn about ourselves by narrowing our focus to the tangible relationships and life experiences that we each encounter. In building these relationships, we help one another find meaning and, in turn, we communicate these shared values as a way of improving our world and ourselves.

The early days of the Clergy Project, when we were a small cloistered community, were a very exciting time for me. It was my first opportunity to speak with peers who up until a few months prior I had no idea existed. I may have lost my community when I left the Church, but here in this virtual assembly it was given back! What mattered to me most from that time and what continues to resonate with me to this day, is that feeling of, "I am not alone." Keeping my loss of faith secret to so many was personally fragmenting. I played a game of continually assessing whether I could share my atheism with this or that person. With the advent of the Clergy Project, a community began to grow that gave me not only the opportunity to speak my truth, but also the validation that is so often granted within the context of peer relationships.

PART II
EXODUS: THE HERETIC NARRATIVE

4

SURVEYING THE NUMBERS

"I look at the faithless with disgust,
because they do not keep your commands."
—Psalm 119:153

When I have an opportunity to speak about the project, I am often asked, "What is a typical Clergy Project member like?" The truth is, though the 600-plus members may have similarities, there really is no typical member. In an effort to provide insight into the membership base, I was granted access to statistical data about Clergy Project members. So as not to erode privacy or anonymity, these statistics, gathered by the project's screening committee, do not divulge any personal information about individual members. Rather, the data tell us a bit about the composition of the project. During the application process, the Clergy Project's screening committee identifies potential members as either "active," meaning they are currently working in ministry, or "alumni," meaning they have left employment in ministry. All other data gathered by the Clergy Project and conveyed herein has been self-reported by individual members. Given that members are encouraged but not required to report this data, a certain percentage of answers for any question are "undeclared."

Active vs. Alumni

Since the very beginning of the project, there has been a consistent ratio of three "alumni" for every one "active" member. We can only speculate as to the reason for this. Possible interpretations include: nonbelieving clergy who have left religious employment find it easier to identify as a nonbeliever than do nonbelieving clergy who remain active; former nonbelieving clergy look for and discover information about nonbelief in greater numbers than do nonbelieving clergy who are still active; and active clergy who are nonbelievers and who learn about the Clergy Project may decide not to join due to fear of exposure. Some might suggest that there are just not that many nonbelieving clergy. This is a possibility, but an unlikely one. Based on my experience, the experience of other project members, and the statistics related to declining seminary students and retention rates, I do not think that this is the case.

Conservative vs. Liberal

Like the numbers regarding "active" vs. "alumni" members, the percentages of those who identify as either "evangelical/ conservative" or "liberal/mainline" have been quite stable from the beginning. More than one-third of members (35 percent) report an evangelical/conservative affiliation, and one-quarter (25 percent) report a "liberal/mainline" affiliation. The remainder (40 percent) have not declared an affiliation. For the purposes of this study, Roman Catholics have been grouped with mainline denominations, Orthodox Christians and Muslims have been categorized as conservatives, and Jewish members have been assigned to either category depending upon their level of orthodoxy.

Why are there consistently more conservatives than liberals as members of the project? Based on anecdotal information, conservative members are expected to adhere to stricter beliefs, and as such are more inclined to have an all-or-nothing approach to their faith, while liberals have more room to interpret their beliefs and are not necessarily required to openly profess literal belief in their denominational creed. In other words, those in liberal religions with doubts can fall back on metaphor and nonliteral interpretations of scripture, while those in conservative religions lack this type of flexibility and thus must either accept or reject all scripture. (For a breakdown of religious affiliation among Clergy Project members as a percentage of membership, see table 1.)

Location

Most of the project's members come from English-speaking countries. This is not surprising given that the Clergy Project Web site is in English and that all of the founders, including the fifty-two original members, are from the United States, Canada, or the United Kingdom. Currently, 79 percent of members are from the United States, and another 7 percent come from Australia, Canada, and New Zealand. Another 4 percent come from Europe, including both the United Kingdom and Ireland. There are members who report being from Africa, Asia, South America, and the Middle East, but collectively they represent only 7 percent of the total membership. Nearly one in ten members or 8 percent have not declared a geographic location (see table 2).

Table 1. Religious affiliation of Clergy Project members (by percent)

Anglican/Episcopal	4
Baptist	10
Bible/nondenominational	1
Buddhist	1
Canada, United Church of	1
Catholic	6
Christ, United Church of	1
Jehovah Witness	1
Jewish (all denominations)	1
Lutheran	2
Mennonite	1
Methodist	5
Mormon	1
Muslim (all denominations)	1
Nazarene	1
Orthodox	1
Pentecostal	8
Presbyterian	4
Quaker	1
Salvation Army	1
Scientology	1
Scotland, Church of	1
Seventh Day Adventists	2
Unitarian Universalist	1
Vineyard	1
Wesleyan	1
Wycliffe Translators	1
Other	1
Nondeclared	41

Table 2. Geographic location of Clergy Project members (by percent)

Africa	1
Asia	4
Australia/New Zealand	2
Canada	5
Europe/UK/Ireland	4
Latin/South America	1
Middle East	<1
United States	79
Nondeclared	8

Gender

About 25 percent of members are women. When you examine the stats related to the enrollment of women in seminaries and take into consideration that the phenomenon of female clergy is relatively new, it makes sense why women compose a minority of project members. According to the Center for the Study of Theological Education at Auburn Seminary's special report on the effectiveness of theological schools, published in December 2007, "women are less likely to enter ministry and to stay, and they encounter more obstacles in religious professions." Even so, this percentage is behind the average number of women graduating from schools of theology and seminary, which currently stands at about one in three graduates. If I were to hazard a guess for this discrepancy, speaking as a woman, I would say that, though women are more likely to be disenfranchised by religion, they are more likely to retain their belief. This is likely true for a number of reasons, including social, cultural, economic, and familial pressures. In addition, some cite factors rooted in evolutionary psychology—for example, that women are generally more risk averse than men and that, in most of the world, identifying as a believer in God is safer than identifying as an atheist. Regardless of the reason for the differences in the levels of religiosity between males and females, there is one important point of correspondence worth noting here: enrollment levels of female M.Div. students, like their male counterparts, is trending downward. Further, despite our status as a minority in the group, the female members of the Clergy Project are fully engaged and are active leaders. We come from a variety of backgrounds, with ministers, pastors, rabbis, chaplains, and nuns counted among us.

Sexual Orientation
Ninety-six percent of members did not self-report a sexual orientation, so unfortunately I have no reliable or meaningful data about the percentages of Clergy Project members who identify as straight, lesbian, gay, bisexual, transgendered, or queer. However, as will be discussed in ensuing chapters, many Clergy Project members have said that, as part of their transition away from faith, they gradually shifted from being socially conservative to socially liberal. One of the key factors contributing to this shift relates to their changing views about sexual morality, sexual ethics, and sexual orientation, and increased awareness of and attention to universal rights for all, particularly as relates to women and LBGT individuals.

Although these numbers may shed some light on what a typical Clergy Project member is like, they tell little about why members abandoned their faith. Though no formal questionnaire has been completed on the subject, and the abandonment of faith generally has no single proximate cause, I found in my discussions with other members that our protracted journeys from faith to reason often had similar features, beginning, notably, with questions about the professed authority of religious institutions and the very nature of faith.

5

THINKING THROUGH FAITH

*"Wisdom cries aloud in the street;
in the markets she raises her voice."*
—Proverbs 1:20

I loved going to mass. Walking up the steps of the church I attended every Sunday morning was a comfortable ritual that drew me to the sanctuary. Inside, the atrium consisted of a smattering of stained glass above the entry doors. In the middle of the room stood a large Calcutta marble font, its hue golden, with intricately carved doves chiseled by a long-dead artisan. I would reach out my hand, and the slight movement would ripple the water. Methodically, I made the sign of the cross and reaffirmed the sacrament of my baptism. Each step inside the church called me to focus, to tune out the world, and to draw my attention to the transcendent. The structure of the church echoed this. From the heavens, the formulaic architecture clearly showed the shape of a cross. I loved the idea of God seeing our cruciform offering from on high; it made me think we were clever. Moving into the nave, rows of oak pews filled the space from the entry to the rail at the bema, beyond which stood the altar. It was a single piece of carved golden marble, like the font. The top was draped by a bright green antependium, upon which was embroidered "Pax Christi." My eyes leapt to the back of the church, behind the altar where the tabernacle stood in all its glory—a ten-foot-tall golden warehouse for the transubstantiated bread. This was my Sunday morning ritual. This was the place where I first cultivated a vocation to religious life—where I came for consolation and where now, as a heretic, I no longer wish to tread.

I understand the intimate and intoxicating influence of faith; it lulls anxiety, promising resolution, order, and calm in a world outside of our control. What few believers see is that religion claims authority by preying on our fears, all the while attempting to establish a universal norm that relies heavily on personal narrative, a grand scheme that artificially supports religious presuppositions. But the foundation on which the Church's power relies—faith and authority—is built on unstable ground. Many members of the Clergy Project, when faced with hypocrisy or injustice within their religious tradition, began to question their faith. For me, one incident that negatively and seriously influenced my perception of the Church, and one that I now see as a touchstone for my later doubts, occurred when I was fifteen years old.

You cannot be a Catholic, or a former Catholic, without some opinion on clergy sexual misconduct. Beginning in the late 1980s, a series of sexual abuse scandals made international news, rocking the faith of many Catholics. At the time, people in the Church I attended were shocked, but they ultimately dismissed such horrid events as isolated incidents. No one was willing to imagine the possibility that child abuse was widely prevalent. Nor was anyone willing to admit that the Church would ever attempt to ignore or even hide such a systemic problem.

As a young parishioner, I was among those who never doubted the unassailable goodness and wisdom of the Church and its priests. That all changed in my teenage years, when my diocese in Antigonish Nova Scotia, like countless others around the world, witnessed its own child-abuse scandal. In this instance, my parish priest, Father Claude Richard, along with his twin brother, also a priest, were the abusers. Unlike many other cases, where complaints about a predatory priest led to nothing more than a molesting priest's reassignment to a new parish, both men were formally charged and convicted of indecent assault against minors.

I knew Father Richard. I was one of the altar servers on the rotation for the Sunday morning liturgy. I remember him as always happy to see the youth of the parish. His round face and receding hairline only further disarmed people. He did not look like a predator, but he was one. He often hosted youth events at the parish glebe house. He, along with his brother, would arrange for pizza nights for altar servers; they would put on a little show and delight us with songs and jokes. I do not recall observing anything out of the ordinary at these events. We had no idea that a monster laid beneath his kindly exterior. One day, Father Richard left the parish unexpectedly. I did not at first know why, but several months later, I heard the whispers.

As my diocese began to swarm with stories about Father Richard, his brother, and others, a large sex-abuse scandal erupted in an adjacent diocese, which was covered widely in the news. There were widespread allegations of sexual abuse of children under the care of Christian Brothers at Mount Cashel Orphanage, with approximately three hundred victims coming forward. Bishop Colin Campbell attempted to protect the reputation of the priesthood, his diocese, and the Church by publicly dismissing the accusations made by the victims. In *The Casket*, a community newspaper, he wrote, "If the victims were adolescents, why did they go back to the same situation once there had been one pass or suggestion? Were they cooperating in the matter, or were they true victims?"

Church leaders read this letter from every pulpit, in every church in my diocese. I remember sitting in the pew next to my mother as the bishop's—and, by extension, the Church's— opinions of the victims were made plain to parishioners. Audible gasps could be heard peppered throughout the very still sanctuary. Traumatized by news of the scandal, which included friends and family of those in the pews, people had been waiting for a pastoral and loving message—what they got instead were the angry ramblings of an embattled oligarch completely lacking in empathy. I sat silent in the church, processing what I heard, feeling it echo in my head like an unwelcome thought.

A few months after the bishop issued his horrendous proclamation, my mother sent me to our diocese's summer youth camp for girls. After surveying the run-down cabins and shabby grounds, I did not expect much from this weeklong expedition. The camp was populated by fifty teenage girls, who were each sent to this "Catholic youth ministry" to help encourage and foster their faith. Though we were teenagers with all the obvious distractions, the recent events in the diocese and the comments of the bishop were frequently discussed and privately admonished. Attending the camp was a young blond-haired woman, the target of a predator teacher, who refused to be defined by the circumstances that surrounded her. The story of her attack at the hands of a trusted educator had been splashed all over the local newspapers. Though her identity had been "protected" due to her age, everyone knew who she was. Despite these challenging circumstances, she refused to adhere to the role of victim. Her emotional maturity and refusal to be silenced inspired us.

On Wednesday, the camp administrators announced we would be having a special guest the following day. The camp was abuzz, as we speculated about who would be coming. Just before the dinner bell rang the next day, Bishop Campbell pulled up with his entourage in a black Lincoln. Our excitement immediately dimmed. Smiling broadly, he appeared to be expecting a throng of adoring and diminutive pupils. Camp counselors ushered us into the mess hall with little fanfare. After the meal, they directed us to rearrange the seating into rows and to take a seat.

The bishop went to the lectern to speak to the uncomfortably captive audience. We all stared at him, wondering what his goal was, as he addressed us as "young women." He began prattling on about Jesus, the Church, love, and salvation, all the usual stuff. In the middle of his presentation, the blond survivor stood up; she had a question. The bishop stopped, looking down at her with what appeared to be hopeful expectation. Politely but firmly, she asked him why he had issued such a hateful statement about the victims of predatory priests. He sputtered, his face rapidly transitioning from pale pink to a flustered red. Sucking in his breath, he admonished her, "How dare you ask such a question. Do you not understand that my priests were the victims?" These adolescents were responsible, he charged, scowling, as they were the tempters. I sat there in my rickety chair, stunned.

His outrage at her perceived insubordination reduced him to a vicious, angry man. Gripping the lectern tightly, his hands trembled with rage. His shoulders tensing, he began to ridicule her, saying that she was "too young to understand" and that she had "no right to question his authority or opinions." He was her bishop, after all. At the end of his diatribe, she turned around and walked out on him. The rest of us got up and followed her out the door.

The bishop did not know what to do. For perhaps the first time in his life, he had been confronted by pointed questions that toppled his egotism and ignored his title. We refused to acquiesce to his so-called moral authority, seeing him for what he was, deeply flawed. He lingered on the podium, like an unsure speaker, nervous of a crowd. Outside, we formed a circle and sang, *"We are children, children of the light. We are shining, in the darkness of the night. Hope for this world, joy throughout the land. Touch the hearts of everyone, take everybody's hand."*

While we stood singing, that bitter little man stormed off with his entourage. His comments would continue to haunt him during his remaining years as bishop. In his 2012 obituary, priests described him as "a man of strong views" who ruffled feathers with his statements regarding the sexual abuse of children. Unfortunately, his successor, Bishop Raymond Lahey, who was brought in to broker reconciliation between the diocese and the victims of its predatory priests, was not much better. He was defrocked in 2013 and is now notorious for his conviction for possessing and importing images of child pornography.

As demonstrated time and again, the culture of protectionism in the Roman Catholic Church does not extend to victims of predatory priests. Though a lot of money and countless apologies have been offered, little has been done internally to access and treat the culture that enabled these predators to thrive unrestrictedly. This story is not only one about the hypocrisy of the Church, but also about the control that it extols on the laity. The hierarchy of the Church demands capitulation and subjugation. For generations it has exploited its followers by cultivating a need for its sacraments, holding them in ransom to a desperate laity who have bought into the benefits and power of the Eucharist. Over time, I became aware of this Machiavellian charade, and the slow painful seeping in of this knowledge ultimately forced me to face my doubts—and the nature of faith.

Doubt has been described throughout the thousand-plus years of church literature as the dark night of the soul. Doubt is something that is regularly talked about by the faithful, clergy and laity alike. In seminary, we spent a lot of time talking about it in my pastoral courses, and members of the clergy—in a grand twist of logic—have long held that doubt itself can make your faith stronger. Thomas Merton, an American Benedictine Monk and so-called mystic, wrote, "You are not big enough to accuse the whole age effectively, but let us say you are in dissent. You are in no position to issue commands, but you can speak words of hope. Shall this be the substance of your message? Be human in this most inhuman of ages; guard the image of man for it is the image of God." The experiences shared by members of the Clergy Project reflect this sentiment: faith does indeed ebb and flow. It is as mutable as the seabed during a violent storm. In the case of each project member, however, faith ultimately crashed on the shores of reason, where its remnants morphed into values that do not rely on mysticism in order to float.

Consider briefly the words of some of the Clergy Project members who have detailed their struggles with doubt:

"Stan Bennett," a closeted agnostic who still works as a minister for a mainline denomination

I think it was somewhere in my tenth year of being a minister that I started having doubts, but I was too scared to admit it, so I plunged myself deeper into ministry and became more adamant in my fundamentalist ways. I insisted that since the Bible was completely true, we must believe in miracles and supernatural spiritual gifts, and if we didn't see those things occurring then there must be something lacking in our faith.

I prayed more fervently than ever but no one was ever listening on the other end. I longed to feel the presence of the Holy Spirit but I never did. I looked for some sign that there was a consciousness out there that cared for me deeply, but I have never seen it.

It probably doesn't surprise anyone that I eventually became sick and depressed, at which point the realization that I no longer believed in Jesus hit me hard.

Mary Johnson, a former Missionary of Charity turned secular activist

After I left religious life, I began to see how much my beliefs had been shaped by others telling me what I was supposed to think. I began to see through the holes in religious authority first, especially as I saw so many ways in which religious authorities abused their power. I began to realize how dangerous it was when some people tell others what they should think.

"Sherm," an Orthodox rabbi who is secretly an atheist

Everything about Judaism became more rational. I tried to rationalize everything and shift all religious lessons in the direction of universal morality. I would try to make everything I taught conform to a framework that, to my mind, all rational thinkers would agree with. Eventually, however, one is not able to ignore God and religious spirituality in a religious setting like my community (Orthodox Judaism). So I started to teach almost as I did before I lost faith.

As far as family is concerned, only my wife is aware of my atheism. It has been close to five years now and it is still difficult for her. We do not talk about it that much, but I am very much committed to raising rational, observant Orthodox Jewish children. Our views about what is good in Judaism are very much in line with one another. However, I would be lying if I said that it did not and does not still cause hardships.

Mason Lane, a former pastor turned atheist

Within a few months I quit preaching, moved to another state, and was done with it all. I told members of the congregation individually of my nonbelief but none of them could bring themselves to believe it. It's very threatening when believers learn about one of the flock becoming apostate, and many times more threatening when the apostate is their pastor.

In my own case, I had been encouraged to browse through my own doubts by my spiritual director and others at seminary, but not to fully entertain them. I now realize my own insecurities were being exploited. As a result, I put questions away when they became too overwhelming and returned to prayer. Today, however, I often find myself wondering why and how I ever thought faith was a virtue. Why not tenacity or persistence or intelligence? Why an unrealistic, unrelenting belief in a phantom god—a pretentious all-knowing bully—that manipulates and repudiates, all the while demanding obedience. Faith persists, like an unrelenting drum beat. It permeates our cultures, infecting memes and narratives, defining our politics and social programs, pulling our strings in a malevolent display of sadomasochistic puppeteering.

In many ways, faith is little more than a culturally derived, popular idea. Consider the etymology of the word "Catholic," which comes from the Greek phrase "kata holos," meaning "according to the whole or universal." As active and former religious leaders, Clergy Project members know intimately the lengths religion will go to ensure the universality of its message. Religion perpetuates itself by claiming authority, whether moral or cultural. This attempt to claim superiority is supported by the most superficial of evidences: personal revelation and ancient texts.

To better understand and communicate the values of my faith, I attempted to engage in scholarship so that I might act as a conduit for others. Despite the obvious contradictions in what I learned, the sheer act of acquiring knowledge about my religious tradition did not immediately lead to the deconstruction of my faith. The control belief held over my life speaks to the persistence and pervasiveness of religion, as not only part of our personal narratives, but also as part of our joint or cultural narratives.

In what is now deemed a classic anthropological interpretation of religion, Clifford Geertz stated that "religion is: (1) a system of symbols which acts to (2) establish powerful, pervasive, and long-lasting moods and motivations in men by (3) formulating conceptions of a general order of existence and (4) clothing these conceptions with such an aura of factuality that (5) the moods and motivations seem uniquely realistic." Utilizing Geertz's interpretation, it is understandable why and how religion is easily transmitted and highly impactful, especially during childhood. Religion presupposes an order to perceived—and real—chaos; it quells the mind while instilling its values, which may or may not improve well-being. "Parental, couple, and familial religion are linked with youngsters' pro-social behaviors." Speaking generally, parents rear their children in the tradition with which they are most familiar, and these traditions become a touchstone in which we find meaning and articulate values. Each member of the Clergy Project experienced religion as part of a cultural narrative, and for the majority of members, myself included, this narrative became intertwined with our own sense of identity and empathy. This was in large part due to childhood indoctrination.

The historical context of my own religiosity came from a position of inferiority and subjugation. As a member of the laity, I, like all other Catholics, relied upon tradition. The priest was my intermediary—at least that was what I was told—for all things of a spiritual nature. Given this context, the world outside of the Church, including science and philosophy, was practically alien to me. I vividly remember struggling with concepts in high-school science classes, as they seemed to contradict my faith, and wondering how my religion and science could both be correct. After studying theology, I came to see that it was my faith that was malleable, not the laws of physics. The orthodoxy of my childhood vanished and I enjoyed the exercise of reconstituting my church to fit my personal agenda. When I was a practicing Catholic, I often stretched my imagination by envisioning my own church not as a global oppressor of women but as a segmented community, "a church within a church," that devised its mandate not from the pulpit in Rome but from the roots of liberation theology. I spent many years at the altar of feminist theologians, honoring their articulation of the liberated experience.

The intensive efforts that are needed to sustain faith against the ravages of reason point to the limits of its application. In my experience, rejecting my vocation and my faith was not a movement away from something. It was a motion toward acceptance. It was an acknowledgement of reality and of my goal to stop the influence of wish fulfillment on my articulation of meaning and behavior. It thus saddens me to think that, while many believers have doubts, few of them will see this experience as their intellect and instinct attempting to lead them out of ineffective and dangerous thinking. Indeed, such doubts are instead blamed on the devil or the inherent evil in humanity. This continuous cycle of doubt vs. faith is sustained through the willingness of the believers to stifle their openness to questions and to continue with the exercise of cultivating specks of wisdom gleaned from scripture and theology.

In my experience, and in the experience of many other Clergy Project members, doubt alone was not enough for us to break away from faith. A constellation of other factors contributed to our rejection of faith. While there are arguably as many factors as Clergy Project members, a trinity of factors—specifically, the study of theology, feminist thought, and the struggle for LGBT rights—led me to acknowledge the limits of faith and provided me with the tools to observe and deconstruct the internal architecture of my faith. Many other members of the Clergy Project refer to the importance of these and other deconstructive elements in their final break from faith. In short, once you begin to think about your faith outside of the simple context of belief and, as "Adam" says, "get a peek behind the Wizard's curtain," religion becomes like any other idea, only as strong as its ability to stand up to logic and reason.

6

DRIVING DOUBT: SEMINARY

"Jesus immediately reached out his hand and caught him,
saying to him, 'O man of little faith, why did you doubt?'"
—Matt 14:31

As far back as I can remember, faith was an intricate part of my life, a practice that was determined and cultivated by my mother. As a child, I had experienced a series of illnesses. Each time I recovered my mother interpreted my survival as God's will. This interpretation was communicated to me as though I should recognize the situation as being particularly special or unique. I remember being told more times than I can count that my pain and suffering had brought me nearer to God and that I should be thankful for the opportunity to be so close to Jesus.

I internalized this message from my mother, like any child would. It guided me in my devotion and challenged me to empathize with the crucified Christ and with the suffering of others. It propelled me to read the Bible and ask questions, and, when I was eighteen years old, it led me to the door of a convent. I thought life in the sisterhood may be for me, and so I scheduled a meeting with a nun who was a longtime friend of my mother and frequent visitor to my family's house.

The building was familiar to me; I had been in it many times over the years. It was not the "motherhouse" but a renovated hundred-year-old three-story Georgian that was commissioned as the local residence for the sisters. It had six large flat steps to direct me to the arched double doors. The paint on the doors looked multilayered, with bumps and scrapes associated with its frequent use. A sign in the door window read, "Please ring the bell for assistance." I pushed the round buzzer and waited patiently. Sister Martha came to the door with a broad smile, her greying hair cut in a short bob. She wore a slightly old-fashioned burgundy suit jacket, a plain black A-line knee-length skirt, and practical shoes. I had expected her to invite me inside, but she crossed the threshold and said, "I thought I would take you to lunch."

My mother had dropped me off, so we got in her car and headed to a local dive. We sat down at a secluded table, and she began to ask me questions about my "vocation." Surprisingly, I was very nervous to be having this conversation with someone I had known my whole life. My hands trembled as I tried my best to give her the answers I thought she was seeking. After less than an hour, she stopped asking questions and looked at me in a pensive but kind way and said, "I think you should study some theology before you commit to this decision." As it turned out, these were wise words.

Moving from the role and function of a religious leader to one of a nonbelieving apostate is massive to say the least. For the majority of the believing population, this is a leap that they do not understand and in many instances cannot even envision. One of the reasons for this may be that they are not privy to the knowledge that is revealed in seminary. Though not all members of the Clergy Project attended seminary, a considerable number of us did. For those of us who did attend, embracing the study of theology and biblical scholarship played a significant role in the deconstruction of our subjective religious experiences. My goal here is not to dive into the theological pool, and relish its hot and cold waters, but to provide a peek into the muddled insight of this artificially heady world. What I and other Clergy Project members could not have foreseen early in our seminary education is how the very the tools of theological interpretation would become primary drivers in our burgeoning doubts.

Taking the advice of the good sister, I put my efforts into studying. The first two classes I took as an undergraduate were exciting and eye-opening. They provided me with answers about my faith and gave me permission to stretch the boundaries of understanding. My first class in biblical scholarship laid out the relevant facts regarding the origins of the Bible, including the Old Testament, or Torah, and the New Testament and its synoptic problem. In some ways, it was refreshing that the professor was honest about the history of the text and that he did not sugarcoat the facts. Despite my dependency on Catholicism, I loved this approach. I was given "permission" to understand this holy book, as well as the tools to enable this process. Unlike many of the other students in the class, who were frequently bothered by the details that ran contrary to their religious upbringing, I was unfettered by this problem. In fact, I was blissfully ignorant of it! I took my faith, put it in a "sacred box," and went about my business pursuing the answers that had long evaded me, a textbook definition of cognitive dissonance.

My introductory class to theology similarly expanded the horizons of my religious beliefs. I was given the tools to interpret, access, and reconstitute my faith. Theology had become for me an intellectual exercise, but I remained wholly oblivious to the limits of its application and the extent to which it could be undermined. Nonetheless, I attempted to assert theology's continued relevance in my life by researching social movements such as liberation theology, as defined by Gustavo Gutiérrez and Leonardo Boff.

After completing a bachelor's degree so focused on theology and its application for social justice, I felt compelled to seek out the vocation I had always intended, and so I applied to seminary. At the time, I gave little additional thought to entering a religious order or becoming a sister; I felt that should the spirit move me in that direction, then my path would naturally unfold. Rather, I planned to start in chaplaincy and wait to be guided, confident that my life was being directed and influenced by God. I have heard many other members of the Clergy Project describe their entry into seminary or ministry in the same way.

Entering seminary is, at once, a spiritual calling and a practical vocational choice. Before I started my graduate studies, I had high expectations for the program, and even higher expectations for myself and how this program would challenge and enable me to be of service. Just before my first semester was set to start, however, my father was diagnosed with a malignant brain tumor. I decided to delay the start of my seminary training for a year, so that I could be closer to him. Having just graduated with a bachelor's degree in theology, I quickly found a job working for the Archdiocese of

Halifax. As manager of their Refugee Support Program, one of my responsibilities was to provide nonlegal representation to refugee claimants at their immigration hearings. I also coordinated access to social supports and assistance for the refugees who sought out our help. As a sponsorship agreement holder, the archdiocese had been approved by the federal government to provide services to refugees within its jurisdiction. I was the only staff person in the office, managing a caseload of several hundred refugee claimants.

To say I was naive at that time would be an understatement. I lived and breathed the gospel. I was a companion of Christ, and I felt called to be of service to the Church. Despite being a woman and having had lots of experience being judged as a woman, I failed at the time to appreciate that I would always be seen as a woman first and a minister or chaplain second. Eager to please, I was happy to work long hours with no overtime pay. I took up residence in the church-provided accommodations, at a nearby glebe house. At the time, it was just me—a twenty-three-year-old woman, sharing a three-story residence built for eight priests and brothers with a fifty-six-year-old parish priest. After working all week at the archdiocese, I volunteered time on the weekends at the crumbling 150-year-old church. I sang in the choir, was a Eucharistic minister, and helped organize charity events to help the poor in the neighborhood. I am sure that people talked, but nothing ever happened between the priest and me. We became very good friends, and when he died four years ago, I regretted that I had not reached out to him to talk about my loss of faith.

Still, taking this very demanding job enabled me to be close by during my father's illness and at his death, some five months after his initial diagnosis. My grieving process cemented my desire to return to school and motivated me to fulfill what I saw as my vocation. I believed that the experiences that led me to decide to become a chaplain had been divinely ordained. Whether it was my working for the archdiocese, my time as a youth group leader organizer, or my participation in the active campus ministry, all aspects of my narrative pointed to a life of service in ministry. I felt that I was at the precipice of a life of value and meaning. I gave my all to the Church, and I was a true believer! From time to time, I find myself wishing that I had studied something else, but realistically, I do not have any regrets. Working for the Church and studying theology was indeed an education. I took from it what resonated and have used those experiences to transform my life and articulate my values, just not in the way I had expected when I first began my training.

Most people outside of seminary know little about the formation of clergy and even less about the history of seminaries. Seminaries as we know them today emerged as part of the Roman Catholic Church's Counter-Reformation, beginning in 1545 with the start of the Council of Trent. Prior to the council, the education of nonordered or "secular diocesan" clergy was primarily provided through Cathedral and Monastic schools. These programs functioned similarly to modern-day apprenticeship programs. Augustine of Canterbury (not to be confused with Augustine of Hippo) founded the first Cathedral school in the English-speaking world in 597, only a few short years before his death in 604. Prior, clergy generally belonged to religious orders, and it was through their period of formation at Monastic schools, as novitiate and scholasticate, where they studied to fulfill the necessary requirements to be "brothers" or "priests."

Augustine of Canterbury's contributions, along with the work of Cathedral schools throughout Europe, including Chartres and Utrecht, followed the example set by earlier monastic traditions. The difference, however, was that the Cathedral schools were not linked to religious orders and were the training group for "secular" or diocesan clergy. The Cathedral schools laid much of the foundation for today's universities, instituting theology as the pinnacle of academic disciplines. By the time the Council of Trent closed in 1563, the Church had tied up many of the loose ends left by the previous eighteen ecumenical councils, and the role and functions of universities, as the educators of clergy and the domain of theology, was cemented.

Between the first Council of Nicaea in 325 and the Second Vatican Council in 1965, the Church, its doctrines, and its magisterium evolved to address threats to apostolic authority, both real and imagined. The laborious work of manufacturing and maintaining magisterium was meant to ensure the Church's continued relevance in light of emerging epistemologies and the transformative power of scientific discovery. The growth of humankind's knowledge about the natural world placed the Church in a difficult position. Gone were the days when the Church could silence dissenters, as it did with Giordano Bruno, or force a recantation, as in the example of Galileo Galilei. By the time of the Second Vatican Council, the Church had all but given up its old ways of influence, as when it officially abolished the *Index Librorum Prohibitorum,* or List of Prohibited Books, in 1966. This step could unofficially be seen as the Church's begrudging acknowledgment of its growing irrelevance in the new world order.

One component that often gets overlooked when the waning influence of the Church and religion is considered is the impact of epistemology and the growing warehouse of knowledge that influenced the academic inner workings of both theology and biblical scholarship. Seminary provides an intimate view into this dynamic. After countless hours accessing and wrestling with theological discourse, I can state assuredly that the language and application of religious and biblical scholarship central to the formation of clergy in Catholic and Mainline Protestant schools of theology would be barely recognizable as Christianity to the majority of believers sitting in the pews. Though much time is devoted in seminaries to understanding and cultivating the relationship between faith and reason, little dialogue is given to the question: can faith withstand the onslaught of reason?

The influence of evidence- and reason-based disciplines have infiltrated theology so much that, in many ways, theology today relies on scientific methodology and Enlightenment philosophy to inform its academic development. These methodologies, which allow us to filter our collective human *gnosis*, or knowledge, stand out as alien totems on the religious landscape, where once the previously prevailing world order required no second opinion or intellectual insight. These interdisciplinary tools have been used so successfully that they have mostly dismantled centuries-old paradigms, where everyone knew their place on the "great chain of being."

Human history, and salvation history, as it is understood by the Church, was greatly influenced by Augustine of Hippo, a prolific theologian and philosopher who lamented the inferior nature of man. His own life, detailed thoroughly in his work *Confessions*, was preoccupied predominantly by sin. Salvation history, which links its beginning to the "fall" in the Garden of Eden, is the most notable of Augustine's conclusions. We are fallen, blemished, and unpure, somehow deserving of eternal punishment for the finite amount of sin we kick up during our brief lifetimes.

A classical source of patriarchal anthropology, Augustine greatly influenced the magisterium. His fixation on sin and redemption and his focus on the dichotomy between body and soul followed the example laid out by early Christian Gnostics and the eschatological leanings of the New Testament. Unfortunately, such interpretations, common among other patristic theologians, continue to permeate the more orthodox aspects of the Church, an example of which is the overtly macabre fascination with human suffering as displayed in the crucifix.

The Church, in many ways, resents knowledge that may limit or lessen its authority. Although it made many attempts to quell the Renaissance and Enlightenment, these cultural movements moved forward and produced important advances in anatomy, astronomy, chemistry, mathematics, physics, and philosophy. For example, Immanuel Kant's secular ethics, which the Church condemned, arose in the wake of these movements. This new age of intersecting ideas birthed the concepts of human rights and freedom of speech. Natural-born rights began to erode the authority and subjugation instituted by a feudal church and society. The Church's days as the warehouse of all knowledge were thus numbered.

This openness to new possibilities spurred on new ideologies, discoveries, and socio-political acrobatics, such as the works of Darwin, Nietzsche, Marx, and Freud. These new ideas radically challenged the experience of the "everyman," who had previously been tethered to the Church and its edicts on everything. As profound thinkers of the modern and emerging postmodern era, each had their own particular loathing for organized religion. Nietzsche said, "I call Christianity the one great curse, the one enormous and innermost perversion, the great instinct of revenge for which no means are too petty—I call it the one immortal blemish of mankind."

Years spent tending to theological thought left me fairly muddled in my exertion of what I believed. Existential philosophy and theology made up a large component of my theological training. In part, it influenced my study of moral theology, as I sought to focus the role of social responsibility in the equal light of social justice and the gospel. I made use of codes of ethics, such as the Ten Commandments and the pericope of the Jesus narratives, but all were filtered through my modern understanding of universal human rights. As a result, I had no choice but to grudgingly accept that the problem of evil remained a relevant critique of religion and of moral theology that could not so easily be wiped away by the notion of free will.

To quell these questions, and to assert what I thought of at the time as "reasonable answers," I was directed by my professors to the works of several respected theologians—in particular, those foundational works of Paul Tillich, who influenced my thinking with regards to the problem of ontology (being), and the interpretation of meaning and purpose as exemplified in the functioning of the Catholic Church and its hierarchy. Tillich taught that Christianity was the answer to the existential problem created by the vacuum of ontology. His presupposition for this argument was that there could be no contradiction to a theological answer. As an example of this thinking, Tillich wrote, "it is because the Christian message claims, *a priori,* that the *logos* who became flesh is also the universal *logos* of the Greeks."

His claim is an interesting one, but it fails to live up to the scrutiny of modern biblical scholarship. What do I mean by this? Well, Tillich gleaned his appreciation for "logos," which in Greek philosophy means "discourse" or "reason," from the Gospel of John. This gospel differs from the other three so-called synoptic (meaning together or similar) gospels on several counts. Though the use of the Greek word "logos" in the Gospel of John denotes a Hellenistic influence, the gospel was not written for a Gentile Greek community. The current consensus is that the Gospel of John appears to be the work of a Hellenistic Jewish community. What evidence supports this conclusion? Several similarities have been noted between the Dead Sea Scrolls, written by the Gnostic Jewish Essene community at Qumran, and the the Gospel of John in terms of word usage and language flow. Thus, a majority of scholars today believe that the Hellenistic Jewish community that the Gospel of John was written for lived in Palestine. As a result, the usage of "logos" in the Gospel of John is not the same as the usage of "logos" in Greek philosophy. The two are wildly different in meaning. In the Gospel of John, "logos" refers to the "creative force" by which God made the universe and not "reason." Given this usage, Tillich's interpretation rests, in my opinion, on a misreading of the Bible and is thus incorrect.

A second source of influence for me was Bernard Lonergan. A Jesuit philosopher treated with an almost "God-like" reverence in the circles I inhabited at seminary, Lonergan seemed to hover above the seminary, imbuing the work and spirit of the school. His influential work *Method in Theology* sought to institute a theological empirical system that could be utilized to form consensus and agreement between philosophy and theology. For Lonergan, systematic theology attempts to see the Christian tradition as a whole, which can be understood by studying the interrelationships among all its parts. As a way of understanding this method, I would liken it to your elbow pondering the functioning of your knee and finding similarity and appreciation of said functionality and then assessing these commonalities with other body parts according to the whole body system. This is seemingly a beautiful method, though exceedingly unnecessary. Theologians busy themselves with the work of deciphering every organ, joint, and bone of Christian tradition.

What I am hoping is clear is that both of these theologians utilized scientific methods and epistemological practices with the goal of armoring their disciplines with legitimacy. In my opinion, both failed to see that in utilizing these external methods of interpretation, they have not only pointed out glaring limits in theological thinking but also provided examples of the pervasive labyrinth that is cognitive dissonance.

Faith is a conviction of personal narrative and, as such, it is susceptible to fallacy. In the example of these theologians, I would say their work suffers specifically from an association fallacy. Though attempts are made to utilize interdisciplinary tools to buttress the relevance of faith, as seen in the examples of Tillich and Lonergan, other, more disastrous theological interpretations exist. For example, Diarmuid O'Murchu, in his 1997 book *Quantum Theology*, attempts to marry quantum physics with Christian spirituality, resulting in a convoluted and unsubstantiated thesis that excited the likes of new age spiritualist Deepak Chopra.

If it seems that I am judging theology harshly, it is because I am. Theology allows for an explanation that is tailor-made for the desired outcome. It presupposes the destination, like a bossy GPS, confining you to its singular route, limiting your choices and fanning authority all the while leading you in the wrong direction. It is like an interpreter for a language that is no longer spoken and for one that has lost its cultural currency. In a world overrun by kings and dictators, lords and vassals, theology created order. But today, after the dawn of the Enlightenment and the institutionalization of science and the empirical method, we can see that faith provides no genuine answers to ultimate questions. Science and reason have rightly taken over this domain.

Modern theology seeks to maintain its relevance by relying heavily on multidisciplinary methods to reimagine and reinterpret the meaning and values espoused by faith traditions. Over the course of my studies, I was forced to acknowledge that theology followed a pattern when confronted by the challenge of being unable to deflect rational criticism— specifically, it always ended in an appeal to the authority of the Church, to its history, and to the predominance of faith. After years of having my faith repeatedly beaten against the immutable shore of reason, I was forced to recognize that theology is an intellectually dishonest tool that is used by the faithful not only to support their conclusions but also to repudiate their fear of death and meaninglessness.

Indeed, for most seminary students, one form or another of protectionism is the status quo when it comes to sustaining their faith. Cognitive dissonance abounds as facts, reason, and even clear thinking are annexed, all with the goal of shielding belief from valid and thorough critique. Studying theology gives seminary students all the ammunition needed to deconstruct, dismantle, and label outdated tenets of their faith. What they are left with is a shredded ideology that cannot withstand even the most gentle of criticisms before it has to transform into yet another interpretation of meaning. The constant in this exercise is the individuals' desire to sustain or resuscitate their faith—to keep their faith from sinking and to prevent themselves from ending up on the dark, isolated shores of nihilism. Fear of the unknown and fear of irrelevancy become part of the personal narrative that plays out, as a world without god becomes synonymous with a world without meaning. It has been my experience that, for many believers, fear of this very situation, and the inability to accurately reflect on their own role in manufacturing this internal crisis, is what continues to ensnare them in their faith.

Belief is an artifice of self-delusion, and a sad commentary on our inability to move past our intellectual adolescence and to accept reality. Failure to acknowledge our role as architect and procurer of the beliefs, values, and ideas that we espouse is the proverbial elephant in the room. This is the environment in which students at seminary find themselves. Thoughts are quarantined as dialogue on doubt is shut down. This goes not just for the students, but also for the theologians themselves. Shortly after I became a member of the Clergy Project, I reached out to a liberal professor from seminary and asked him what his opinion was on clergy losing their faith. His response was abrupt and to the point, "I have no opinion on the subject." Somehow, I don't buy that.

The time has come for theology to acknowledge that it cannot satisfactorily respond to the thoughtful critique of reason, to recognize that religious experience is part of a subjective narrative, and to cease its attempts to repudiate critique based on this subjectivity. I do not want believers to feel hopeless or to lose purpose. Instead, I hope for a "miracle" of sorts—that they too will see that their beliefs are simply value statements and that many of these values are universal. I would challenge them to look to ethics and universal human rights as the backbone of their ideologies and to pack away outdated thinking that does little to improve well-being for our communities, for our planet, or for ourselves.

7

DECONSTRUCTING RELIGION: FEMINISM

*"Let a woman learn in silence with full submission.
I permit no woman to teach or to have authority over a man;
she is to keep silent."*
—1 Timothy 2:11–15

One fact that I could not avoid in seminary was that I am a woman. Despite higher enrollment of laywomen in Catholic seminary interested in working in chaplaincy and spiritual direction relative to the past, females were clearly outnumbered by males among my student peers. Real and perceived stigmas are par for the course when you are the minority. While my female colleagues attending Protestant seminaries were preparing for ordination, I was assessing my role as a helper and second-class citizen in the Catholic Church. I routinely encountered sexism and, in a search for consolation, found myself reading increasingly "radicalized" feminist theologians. Utilizing a somewhat outdated modus operandi, the "hermeneutic of suspicion," I attempted to emulate the methods of notable thinkers of the late nineteenth and early twentieth century, such as Marx, Nietzsche, and Freud.

The term hermeneutic of suspicion, first coined by philosopher Paul Ricoeur, attempts to imbue theological and biblical scholarship with a method that embraces objectivity and suspicion. In the context of feminist liberation theology, the Bible and church history are deconstructed and assessed for authenticity specific to the liberation of women—for example, through biblical scholarship that focuses on the egalitarian relationships that Jesus had with women such as Mary Magdalene, or on the history of persecution of early Christian martyrs like Perpetua and Felicity and the roles that these women played in the leadership of the early Church.

Deconstructionist methods, like feminism, are thought by most to have nihilistic tendencies, with some viewing them as forms of nihilism. Before I left the Church, I found myself vacillating on this high wire of thought. I remained a Christian not because of my beliefs, which at the time were extremely liberal and in no way, shape, or form resembled the tenets of faith, but because of my fear of the abyss. As artificially precarious as it sounds, my inability to forgo religion not only held me hostage to fear of the unknown, but also led to my continued subjugation as a woman. Feminism theology, for a time, gave me confidence that I could scale religion's misogynist chasm and find on the other side unity and peace. Eventually I came to accept that my hoped-for vision of egalitarianism in the Church and religion was an illusion.

Today many feminist theologians continue the conversation with the Church and its ideological stance on women, much like Mary Daly during her long career as a theologian. They demand dialogue and reworking of God in relation to all of creation. I have long since given up on this idea, and for them I feel sadness for their seemingly never-ending game of advance and decline within the Church. Though Daly had many valid points regarding the reality of systemic subjection of women, her ideas and critique unfortunately tended to be warped by her legitimate but unadulterated anger. Consider briefly this line from her essay "Radical Feminism" in the October 2001 issue of *Philosophy Now,*

> A society manufactured and controlled by males. A society in which every legitimate institution is entirely in the hands of males and a few selected henchwomen. A society which is characterized by oppression, repression, depression, narcissism, cruelty, racism, classism, ageism, speciesism, objectification, sadomasochism, necrophilia, joyless society rule by Godfather, Son and Company; society fixated on proliferation, propaganda, procreation and bent on the destruction of all life.

In my graduate thesis I attempted to find some resolution to this crisis—to the misogyny and sexism—but in the end I was left with the choice of either continuing to foster the illusion of lost-and-found egalitarianism in the Church, or moving on from the construction of church and of god and toward independent thought and healthy self-esteem. In my thesis, or as I now think of it, my "Dear John" letter to the Church, I wrote: "In this hostile atmosphere, many leave the Church. As an individual who has also done so, I can understand the overall frustration and anger at the hypocrisy of Rome. . . . I can find no redeeming qualities in the present-day gallery of Pharisees and their imperialist chain of being."

My conclusions, based on readings of feminist theologians like Mary Daly and Rosemary Radford Reuther, freethinkers like Elizabeth Cady Stanton, and even the somewhat unlikely radical mystics Hildegard of Binghen and Julian of Norwich, would have been deemed damnable a century ago; some may still consider them so. But what has changed is that the rights of ideas, of which religion is one, are secondary to those of the individual rights of people. The women's rights movement, or, more simply, feminism, has contributed to this change.

Feminism has had two major waves, the first occurring in the nineteenth century, which focused primarily on women's right to vote, and the second occurring in the 1960s, 1970s, and 1980s. These two waves, though separated by generations, have both contributed to the upending of religious authority in their own way. Stanton put it quite aptly when she wrote:

> The Bible teaches that woman brought sin and death into the world, that she precipitated the fall of the race, that she was arraigned before the judgment seat of heaven, tried, condemned, and sentenced. Marriage for her was to be a condition of bondage, maternity a period of suffering and anguish and in silence and subjection, she was to play the role of a dependent on a man's bounty for all her material wants, and for all the information she might desire on the vital questions of the hour, she was commanded to ask her husband at home.

Stanton was not only an early leader of the first-wave women's liberation movement; she was also a biblical scholar in her own right. Propelled by her desire to establish liberation for women and for African Americans seeking abolition to slavery, Stanton was a persistent voice in nineteenth-century American politics. Despite her apparent isolation as a mother of seven children living in upstate New York, she was published widely and, in 1848, Stanton called North America's first women's rights convention, where she presented a Declaration of Sentiments, using the Declaration of Independence as her model. Though Stanton was a strong voice for the suffrage cause, she eventually lost her position within the Women's Suffrage Association after publication of her two-part book, *The Women's Bible*, which challenged religious orthodoxy about the place of women relative to men. Many members of the suffrage movement feared her continued association with the movement would entice further criticism from church and state concerning the rights of women and thus denounced her and the work.

The second wave of feminism took more than a hundred years to reach fruition in the 1960s, morphing from the civil rights protests in the United States, student protests around the world, and women's rebellion against the status quo. Out of this personal-communal struggle for justice, two types of women's groups appeared: the small, informal women's liberation groups, which were first formed by female students active in the civil rights movement, and radical political organizations. These groups emphasized self-awareness and open discussion to combat discrimination and to establish greater equality between men and women. One of the most influential and well-known political organizations, the National Organization for Women's Rights (NOW), was formed in 1966 to fight against sexual discrimination.

These radical changes in politics and cultural identity triggered changes and discussion throughout society. During the development of the Second Vatican Council, for example, feminist voices emerged from within the Church, openly critiquing various Church policies and practices. The Second Vatican Council obviously did not overturn the patriarchy that is the Roman Catholic Church, but it did open up the possibility for dialogue. As theological schools began to open their doors to female religious and lay students, the influx of women led to the exploration of ideas about religion and gender that had not been openly expressed since the days of Elizabeth Cady Stanton.

In 1968, three years after the Second Vatican Council closed under Pope Paul VI, Mary Daly's *The Church and the Second Sex* was published. Deemed by many as sensationalized, it called on all women to live the spirit of Vatican II and "to act as her conscience dictated." The Church and academia did not think so highly of Daly's book, and she was promptly fired from her position at Boston College. However, after the school became aware of the book's enormous popularity, Daly was rehired and eventually offered a tenured position. At a most crucial moment in recent Church history, she managed to express the struggle and frustration felt by many women in the Church, particularly in light of second-wave feminism. She wrote, "Radical women always have bad press. Why wouldn't you if you are attacking the prevailing order ... we live in a reversal society, for example the idea that Eve came from Adam, is a reversal, its ridiculous ... it is contrary to biology. But with that myth in mind, people can justify somehow the idea that God is male. And therefore, that male is God."

The word that leaps off the page in this quote is Mary Daly's use of the word "myth." Reading her book in conjunction with exegetical analysis of the Old and New Testaments cemented the reality that I had ignored: this "holy book" was a fabrication, a cultural narrative that only truly reflected the mores and values of the people who wrote it. As such, it is a wholly inadequate resource for humanity in the twenty-first century. Once that realization sunk in, I acknowledged that I was architect of this thing or idea that I called God.

Despite the influence that Daly had on my "god thinking," I was unable or unwilling to participate in the creation of my own existential anthropology of theology. The idea of constructing an argument for egalitarianism in the Church and community only to have it debased and ignored by an egotistical patriarchy drew me to the edge of nihilism—the embrace of meaningless stared back at me from the abyss.

When I think back on my crisis of faith, I see that in shedding my belief, I had to recognize my complacency in the construction of my deity. If I were to reinterpret this period within the context of Trinitarian theology, I would say that "god" is a concept, a paradigm, and a narrative and, as such, is imbued with meaning by its fractured designer, humankind. Feminist theology challenged me to peel away the layers of faith, to deconstruct the fallacies that were represented in the egotism of the Church, and to scrutinize it under the harsh gaze of a hermeneutic of suspicion.

8

TRANSFORMING VALUES: LGBT RIGHTS

"Be ashamed of sexual immorality."
—Sirach 41:17

Homosexuality refers to relations between men or between women who experience an exclusive or predominant sexual attraction toward persons of the same sex. It has taken a great variety of forms through the centuries and in different cultures. Its psychological genesis remains largely unexplained. Basing itself on Sacred Scripture, this presents homosexual acts as acts of grave depravity. Tradition has always declared, "homosexual acts are intrinsically disordered." They are contrary to the natural law. They close the sexual act to the gift of life. They do not proceed from a genuine affective and sexual complementarity. Under no circumstances can they be approved.

This excerpt, taken from the Catechism of the Catholic Church, succinctly sums up the position of the Church with regard to homosexuality. Christianity, including Catholicism, like most otherworldly religions, seeks to corner the market on sexual morality. This habit of legalizing sexual dos and don'ts most definitely predates the formation of the Torah. However, the current incarnations of sexual policing remain and are contributing factors to rampant sexual discrimination and homophobia.

One can easily follow the threads of homophobia through the language and stories of the Bible, but as argued in the last chapter on feminism, many theologians are working to deconstruct and reinvigorate religion to reflect current and emerging social mores and values. With regard to homosexuality, much of this work began in the 1990s with the emergence of "queer theology." Queer theology begins with an assumption that gender nonconformity and gay and lesbian desire have always been present in human history, including in the Bible. It is a way of unraveling structures and stories that have been oppressive. It is also a way of understanding the Bible as a source of stories about radical love. This dynamic of back and forth, between deconstructionist, agenda-pushing theologians and the entrenched traditionalists, does not really play out in the public sphere, but instead becomes part of the debate in schools of theology. Responses to the debate involve either reforming belief or mounting a counterinsurgency against the corrupters of a more traditional interpretation of belief. The mass torture and extermination of dissenters may have ended, but the Reformation has not.

When it comes to the influence of the gay liberation movement, we see a systematically maligned out-group that has recently made successful inroads into the mainstream. This transition from a much-hated and discriminated-against group to a marginally hated and less-discriminated-against group has resulted from enormous efforts within the gay community, including a refusal to live "in the closet." Gay rights have become the present incarnation of civil rights. With the institutionalization of gay rights such as marriage equality into law, these rights become enshrined as universal.

So, what does all this have to do with theology? As you read in previous chapters, the nature of theology itself is a contributing factor to the erosion of belief among clergy. One of the major reasons for this is the variety of liberation theologies that seek to deconstruct a centralized authority in favor of subjective out-group experience. For example, one prominent queer theologian, Marcella Maria Althaus-Reid, sought to mix Latin American liberation theology with a woman-positive, queer-positive, and sex-positive reading of biblical mythologies. Obviously, this type of theology is not what gets communicated from the pulpit, but it does trickle down and become part of the theological lexicon.

Many members of the Clergy Project, particularly those from conservative backgrounds, have indicated that their negative opinions regarding homosexuality eroded as they transformed from conservative believer, to socially liberal believer, to nonbeliever. In many cases, the increased visibility of the gay rights movement and greater exposure to gay individuals triggered this very transformation. Further, a number of Clergy Project members themselves identify as part of the LGBT community. Each of these individuals experienced a disconnect between personal identity and the demands for capitulation to religious authority.

To help illustrate the common transition from conservative believer to socially liberal nonbeliever, I interviewed Robert Parham, a minister of music whose research into gay issues contributed to his loss of faith. To help me understand the difficult challenges faced by gay clergy, I interviewed Tom

Mayhall Rastrelli, a Clergy Project member who told me about his experience transitioning from a closeted gay priest to an openly gay humanist.

Robert Parham

I understand you felt called to ministry at the age of sixteen and by eighteen you were licensed as a minister of the gospel in the Southern Baptist Church. What else can you tell me about your background in Ministry?
For thirteen years, I devoted my life to ministering to people through youth ministry and music. I had planned on earning my master of divinity but was less than impressed with the seminary, and ended up forgoing the M.Div. for a master's degree in counseling. My decision was based on countless attempts to counsel teenagers and parents using the only skills I had. Basically, I used the Bible as the ultimate authority and source of answers to any of life's problems, but found that there are many issues in life for which the Bible is either silent or insufficient.

When and how did you begin to question your faith?
I did not know it at the time, but the decision to change degrees was the beginning of the end of my belief in God. As part of the requirements of my course work, I was tasked with challenging my biases toward oppressed groups. Each student had to select a group that we thought would be the most challenging for us to work with if someone from that group walked into our counseling office for help. The list included women, people of color, the elderly, people with disabilities, people from other religious traditions, and homosexuals. I knew immediately what group would present the biggest challenge for me, so I selected homosexuals.

My biases toward the gay and lesbian community at the time were based on my religious beliefs, which were formed on my belief that the Bible was the inerrant and infallible word of God. At that time I believed that homosexuality was a lifestyle choice made by a person who did not have a personal relationship with God. My work in ministry and the theology that dictated my context stated that homosexuals were sinners who, if they did not repent and change their lifestyle, would go to hell when they die and spend eternity in torment.

This project, which included three assignments of increasing difficulty, would cause me to feel the most uncomfortable that I have ever felt in my life. I knew that I would have to balance this experience in light of my beliefs. The first assignment required me to disclose, in writing, what my biases were, what they were based on, and what past experiences I had had with gays and lesbians. I wrote about the time, as a fourteen-year-old, that a new friend asked me to sexually act out with him during a sleepover. I wrote about how I avoided what I considered a very sinful behavior and then ended the friendship. The second assignment required me to either watch a movie or read a book that would be informative about gays and lesbians. I will never forget how nervous I was walking into a small video rental store on the Southside of Birmingham and asking for help finding a video. I felt compelled to tell the young man working there that I needed it for a class project. I certainly didn't want anyone I knew to see me enter this store. The movie was an Australian film titled The Sum of Us *and starred a very young Russell Crowe. It made an impression on me, as it provided some insight into the lives of people who are gay and the impact this can have on relationships in the family, as well as how it can paint a target on your back in the community.*

The final assignment was to interview someone from my chosen group. In addition to serving in a small church as the minister of music, I was also painting apartments, houses, and condos in order to pay for graduate school. I had painted a condo for a guy who I had figured out was gay, so I took a chance and called him to see if he would be willing to be interviewed. Not only was he willing, he invited me over for dinner. I have to be honest and say that what made me feel so uncomfortable at the time was that I felt like I was on a date.

Aside from the very pleasant meal and casual conversation that we had, I was struck by how eager this person was to share his story with me. He spoke of childhood fears of what his sexual feelings meant. He spoke of the challenges of coming out to his family and friends. He spoke of the love he shared with his partner of seven years and the heartache he experienced when that relationship ended. He spoke of his chosen career and the fear of being terminated if it was discovered that he was gay. I was enlightened by his story. Enlightened to how similar we are versus how different we are. In fact, the differences were few and primarily centered on one thing . . . that we love. Not how we love or whether or not our love is real, but simply the gender of the people we are sexually attracted to.

Can you tell me more about how this experience influences your thoughts related to your faith?
What struck me most during this monumental evening was the struggle I had in answering a simple question that this man asked. Hearing all that I had heard that night, knowing the heartache and pain, the fear of rejection, the fear of the consequences of being outed, the ridicule, the self-loathing generated from the sociocultural programming he was raised with, why in the world would anyone choose this lifestyle?

My thinking was challenged in a way it had never been challenged before in that for the first time I was willing to entertain the idea that the Bible could be wrong about something. For the first time I *sought information outside of religious literature and religious dogma in order to gain knowledge about a subject that could have eternal implications. I began to read the scientific literature available at the time and to read the work of more progressive Christian thinkers, like John Shelby Spong.*

I also began to reflect on a close friendship with a former minister who had confided in me that he was gay. I listened, as a good friend should, as he told me of his struggles with his relationship with his wife, with his ministry, with his childhood abuse, with his conservative Christian faith, with stress-induced medical problems, with severe depression, and even with suicide. My friend was emotionally and mentally tortured due to the conflict he lived with regarding his undeniable sexual orientation and his religious beliefs.

Eventually, I gave myself the opportunity to sit with the doubt I was experiencing, and to embark on a search for answers no matter where that search led me. Gradually, I transitioned from a very conservative, Bible-believing Christian to a more moderate and eventually very progressive, liberal Christian. I could no longer accept the Bible as the inerrant and infallible word of God in light of the overwhelming evidence that proved otherwise. But I wasn't ready to give up my belief altogether, at least not yet.

What happened that pushed you further outside of your comfort zone?

Once I finished my graduate degree in counseling and took my first full-time job as a therapist/case manager in Memphis, Tennessee, I continued to serve as a bi-vocational, part-time minister of music in a small congregation. I had decided that my life was no longer directed by some supernatural plan toward full-time ministry. More and more, I began to feel like a hypocrite among the congregation and the pastor with whom I served. I had mixed feelings, because I truly loved the work and the people, but it became harder and harder to hide my true beliefs about certain issues in the church.

I was assisted in my dilemma when I was recruited by a program in Charleston, South Carolina, and resigned from the church to move there. I had met my then future wife while in Charleston, but before I could make a decision about seeking a new ministerial position, we decided to move in together, so that, in my mind, ended any thought of church work. After all, we were living in sin. I never served on staff at a church again. Over the next ten years, I simply drifted away from the church and put all of my emerging doubts about the existence of God on the back burner.

It wasn't until 2008 that I finally faced my doubts and embarked on a new journey of inquiry. I immersed myself in the writings of Richard Dawkins, Daniel Dennett, Sam Harris, Christopher Hitchens, Victor Stenger, and others. The more I read, the more I felt my belief eroding. Logic and the scientific method replaced blind faith. It gave new meaning to the phrase, "I once was blind, but now I see," which I had sung countless times in the Christian anthem, "Amazing Grace."

I remember the moment that I finally admitted to myself and to my wife that I no longer believed in a god. I lay in bed reading the final sentences of Sam Harris's book, The End of Faith. *I closed the book, laid it on the nightstand, rolled over to face my wife, and said, "We need to talk." It was an emotional conversation that involved tears, but one thing I had no doubt about was our love for each other and that nothing really would change as a result of my lack of belief in a god. I was right. Nearly six years later, we are still together and she is closer to my way of thinking than she is to her Catholic upbringing.*

What have you gained since letting go of your faith?
Being an atheist has brought about even more myth-busting in my life. All of the ideas I had about people who didn't believe in God

completely fell apart. In fact, I feel that my life is more abundant and more joyous now than it ever was as a Christian. I am free to embrace reality and to create my own purpose and meaning in life. I have been asked what gives my life meaning several times since coming out as an atheist. It's quite simple really. My purpose in life is to be the best husband, father, friend, and therapist that I can be. This is what gives my life meaning, knowing that for all of these people in my life, I am important to them. I contribute to their happiness, which in turn brings me happiness.

What is your motivation for doing the work you do with the Clergy Project?

When I speak to different groups about the Clergy Project, I speak about the many ways in which our private-forum members have suffered as a result of giving up their belief in a god. Yes, my deconversion was emotionally painful, and yes, coming out to my family, especially my mother, was difficult. However, I transitioned smoothly into a secular career. My wife did not leave me. My children did not reject me. My friends did not abandon me. I did not lose my house. I did not go bankrupt. My interest and involvement with the Clergy Project was not so that I could receive support or encouragement. I became involved because I saw another way to bring meaning and purpose to my life, another way to help others who may not have been as fortunate as I was in transitioning out of the ministry.

Tom Mayhall Rastrelli

When and how did you begin to question your faith?

It started in the seminary's elevator, something about the Boston Globe, Cardinal Law, *and priests sexually abusing children. I ignored the first few mumbles. I couldn't be distracted. My comprehensive exams, the capstone of six years of seminary, were weeks away. As I immersed myself in the great Christological heresies, politics, anathemas, and holy wars of two millennia of Christendom, the murmurs of January 2002 grew into a cacophony.*

Abuse headlines spread throughout the national media like the plague. Plaintiffs testified. Priests fell. Bishops denied. People prayed for justice for the victims. Others prayed for the protection of their holy priests from greedy opportunists who couldn't forgive and forget. Progressives blamed the archaic sexual repression of celibacy. Conservatives blamed the "gay subculture" of the seminaries. I was gay. I was celibate. I was a victim of sexual abuse.

I felt as if the members of the Church that had "formed" me to be one of its leaders were attacking me from every angle. As the days passed, the mounting allegations, confusion, sadness, anger, and shame metastasized to the serenity and security of my vocation. My ordination was five months away, and I doubted, not my faith in God but the Church.

That's where it started, my adult transition out of faith. That was when I stopped believing the elder generation of priests who warned me against coming out and taught me that not being honest about my sexuality or other internal ecclesial matters wasn't lying if the person seeking the information didn't have the "right" to it. I considered leaving seminary, but there were too many people to disappoint. I was still drinking the Catholic Kool-Aid, the myth that I could change the Church from within, that Church teachings would evolve with the times, that female, married, and openly gay priests were just around the corner, that the Church needed "healthy" and "sexually celibate" (closeted) gay priests to provide role models for young Catholics, and that my generation of priests could right the wrongs of the past. I had to believe it would get better, or my life was a lie.

Can you tell me more about other factors that influenced your decision making?

Two years of scandal and priesthood later, I drove toward the frozen Mississippi River. My plan was to drive onto the ice until it broke and I drowned. I'd just exposed the priest and mentor who sexually assaulted me during confession when I was in college. For two years after, he exploited his knowledge of my being gay to his sexual benefit. In the years that followed, I observed him grooming other possible victims. After hearing this, the archbishop had ordered my obedience and silence. A few blocks from the frozen shore, I stopped. I sobbed. I called a brother priest, who talked me down. I had another option: leave. Four months later, I stood behind the altar consecrating the bread and wine during my last Mass. I no longer believed in transubstantiation, the virgin birth, or the corrupt bishops' authority. I packed up, left the parish, and checked myself into a six-month residency program at the Southdown Institute, where priests, nuns, and ministers retreat for healing after they've been destroyed by their respective churches.

I did not hide my gayness at Southdown. For the first time, I developed a group of out-of-the-closet peers; nearly all the priests there were gay. In group therapy sessions and personal conversations, I witnessed the psychological and developmental violence wreaked upon gay priests by "Holy Mother Church": depression, compulsion, suicidal ideation, addiction, personality disorder, repressed wrath, and shame. We preached, "The truth will set you free," but lived in a Church that required us to conceal our "God-given" nature, because homosexuality was "intrinsically disordered." Our benevolent, omnipotent, and perfect "Father" had created us in "His Triune image" and as relational/sexual beings made to love. But to act upon our homosexual love was gravely sinful. I could no longer ignore the cognitive dissonance of my faith. Luke 11:11–12 reverberated in my head: "What father among you would hand his son a snake when he *asks for a fish? Or hand him a scorpion when he asks for an egg?" I could no longer believe in a god that had given so many of us snakes and scorpions. Either the god of the Christian scriptures was a sadist unworthy of my belief, or scripture's homophobic authors had gotten it wrong and divine revelation was bullshit.*

What help or resources did you have when you left?
With the help of therapists, I underwent cognitive behavioral therapy (CBT). The psychological exercises of CBT unmasked the underlying causes of my depression. These were my psychological distortions or "myths" that I'd come to believe about myself, such as, I'm bad, I'm stupid, I don't deserve happiness, I'm a failure, and I'm disordered. CBT was a psychological Ockham's razor. As I cut away at my cognitive distortions, I realized that most of them were tied to religion. I applied CBT to my beliefs. The snake/scorpion dissonance gave way, because "divine revelation" was a human construct. Original sin and the need for salvation were fear-based control mechanisms. I realized that everything the Church had taught me about its conflicting versions of god was grounded in a fear-based distortion. I evolved into an agnostic. My depression subsided. Self-love replaced loathing. Self-reliance replaced fear. A peace that the Church could not give filled my being.

Was there a turning point, when you finally acknowledged that you were an atheist, given the discomfort you indicated with the word?
After regaining my health, I traveled the country searching for a place to begin my new life. Along the way, I waxed philosophical with innkeepers and intimates, fundamentalist Christians and atheists. I remained an agnostic, willing to accept the possible existence of "something more" that most people classified as god. Atheist seemed too absolute, closed-minded even. I was still operating under old

distortions such as, "Atheists believe in nothing," and "There are no atheists in foxholes." Then, I found myself in a "foxhole."

While on a sixteen-mile hike at Point Reyes National Seashore, north of San Francisco, the encroaching tide trapped me on a cliff-lined strand of remote beach. Poor planning and bad directions from locals had landed me in a do-or-die situation. I had to scale the hundred-foot rock face, or hope that I survived the night's high tide that would swallow the beach. If the waves crashing against the rocks didn't kill me, hypothermia would.

I climbed. It was easy—vertical but with plenty of eroded nooks and crannies to grip. Twenty feet from the top, sandy soil and grasses began to cover the smooth rock. The soil layer gave way. My feet dropped. I slid. I threw my chest against the cliff and grasped for anything as my fall accelerated. I jammed my forearm into a hole in the rock and dangled. As I hung from the cliff, my past didn't flash before my eyes. The fear pulsing through my veins didn't drive me to prayer. There were no angels to rescue me. No afterlife would embrace me after the coming fall. I had only my body and this life. Any vestiges of faith in a "something more" crashed against the rusty yellow boulders below. I grabbed the rock. I climbed. I slid. I tried again, until I made it to the top an atheist.

As the next few years passed, I read Richard Dawkins, Christopher Hitchens, Dan Savage, and other nonbelievers. I shed my distortions about atheism and embraced this aspect of my identity. It wasn't easy. I lost more friends and close family relationships by coming out atheist than I did coming out gay.

PART III
REVELATION: THE NARRATIVE OF NOW

9

SEARCHING FOR A NEW CALLING

"And he appointed twelve, whom he also named apostles,
to be with him, and to be sent out to proclaim the message."
—Mark 3:14

The relationships that have been built and fostered as a result of the Clergy Project have become very important to me. We have reached out to one another, embracing our diversity and our sameness. This community has allowed me not only to help my peers who are in need but also to help myself, as I participate in the type of positive process that motivated me to go into chaplaincy in the first place. I see my struggles, my successes, and myself in my peers. For the majority of Clergy Project members, finding a way out of active ministry is the goal once they realize they have lost their faith. Finding meaning and employment outside of ministry enables Clergy Project members to live authentically and allows them to embrace all aspects of their life and history.

A career in ministry is in some ways similar to any other.

It is work that is most often described as altruistic, a job where doing well is more important than making money. The concept and application of relationships define work in ministry and, as such, leadership and collaboration become defining principles. Due to this, many members of the project have found employment outside of religion in a number of helping professions.

For clergy who have lost their faith, the context of working in an environment with such structured and ethical dimensions can be burdensome. For most of us, rejecting our "call" or vocation is principally about forgoing belief. It does not take away from our motivation to do good work and to have a positive impact in our communities and on our world. In this respect, humanism becomes the motivating factor both for those nonbelieving clergy who remain in ministry and for those who move on to so-called secular careers.

Former evangelical minister Jerry DeWitt, after coming out as a member of the Clergy Project, famously said about humanism, "Skepticism is my nature, freethought is my methodology, agnosticism is my conclusion, atheism is my opinion, and humanism is my motivation." We members of the project may have, in our own way, rejected our faith traditions, but what we have retained is our hope for humanity and the world, and we do our utmost to extend this well-being to the rest of the planet. The challenge, for many, is to determine how to put this new worldview into practice.

From practically the beginning of the project, there were discussions about the challenges of finding employment outside of ministry. Leaving a job in ministry is unlike any other career change. Not only are there feelings of isolation, but there are also fears about how to communicate one's skills in ministry to another job. Most members who had already left church work detailed a long arduous journey to find employment outside of religion. Many, if not most, of them returned to school, seeking degrees in psychology, social work, business administration, and computer science. It was clear from our discussions that still-active clergy members needed access to resources that could help them find sustainable employment outside of ministry. Thus, about a month after the project launched, I proposed that a group of us brainstorm some possible solutions to employment needs.

I remember my anticipation at having an opportunity to hear the voices of these new friends whom I only knew from their avatars and screen names. We set up an off-forum meeting via teleconference, and though we were unable to see one another, listening to each other's voices introduced a whole new level of urgency to the needs of the members. Though the forum provided a huge relief to members who had previously been isolated, the reality was that active clergy had very tangible needs, and the highest priority was finding sustainable employment for those who needed it.

Led by "Adam," we discussed creating a job board, finding a recruiter to help our members, investigating programs that could help our members find employment outside of the church, and even starting up a business to employ project members. That first meeting mostly provided us an opportunity to share, and it was the first step toward the work that lay outside of the forum. This meeting also cemented friendships as the stories shared highlighted the seriousness of the struggle of our members.

We were bubbling with ideas but had little in the way of resources to make anything happen. At that time, very few people knew of the project's existence, and we weren't sure we were ready yet to let the world know we were here.

We realized that we would have to be prepared before we attempted any next steps, and so we formed a working group to plan the launch of a public Web page where media, members of the public, and nonbelieving clergy could go to find out more about the project. Sounds like a pretty easy thing to do, but in reality, it took our group of planners a lot of time to get things ready for the launch.

By October 2011, we were ready with a public Web page that included an application page for nonbelieving clergy. Linda LaScola and I worked to create an intake process and to gather volunteers to act as screeners, so we were ready for a flood of new applicants. Arguably, the most important component of being a member of the Clergy Project is the ability to listen. Indeed, the primary goal of the Clergy Project is not to deconstruct religion, nor to offer grants or services, but to hear the challenges that our members are facing and to instill in them the knowledge that they have been heard. The importance of listening applies to the screening process as well. Part of being heard is knowing that you matter, that your experience has meaning, and that your story resonates with your peers—a seemingly simple goal, but one that really counts.

As anticipated, after the launch of our public page, the Clergy Project began to garner interest from the media. Many of the first interviews were done with "Adam," the project's first member and then an active evangelical minister. "Adam" was the first person I met on the forum. Although I did not then know his real name, what he sounded like, or his location, I recognized that he, like myself, understood the fear that is inherent with being found out as a heretic. Though he was trapped in the pulpit, confined by the challenges of finding employment outside of ministry and the expectations of his family and community, he remained hopeful. His first message to me spoke of his anticipation for our emergent community, and for a future where he could escape the pressure of spiritual leadership. Listening to his story I saw myself and the long road that I had trudged to find a career outside of ministry. I remembered the fear, the isolation, and the insecurity that I felt when I left, and I wanted to continue to do what I could to help "Adam" and the other members of the project. It occurred to me that the Clergy Project forum, though virtual, had become as real to me as any church community, and I saw clearly that being a member was not only about what you received, but also about what you could contribute.

As expected, the public Web site and the media exposure led to a spike in new members, as the project began to emerge as a secular phenomenon. Both the Richard Dawkins Foundation for Reason and Science and the Freedom From Religion Foundation began accepting donations on behalf of the Clergy Project, which remains a project of both organizations. One generous donation in particular finally enabled us to help those clergy like "Adam" who needed help on the job front.

On February 19, 2013, the Clergy Project announced a new Employment Transition Program to help project members find employment outside of ministry. This new program was made possible by a $100,000 grant from the Stiefel Freethought Foundation. Announcing the donation, Todd Stiefel, the organization's founder and president, said, "With this donation, my foundation hopes to help formerly religious clergy find secular employment. These clergy men and women will no longer have to put the priority of feeding their family above their desire to stop preaching what they no longer believe. Additionally, this is an investment in the next great leaders of the freethought movement because of the incredible skills such as community building, support, and management that these clergypersons bring with them."

As the then acting executive director of the Clergy Project, I had the privilege of working with Todd in recruiting RiseSmart, an outplacement and career transition company, to provide Clergy Project members with assistance finding employment outside of ministry. The company supported our goals and objectives and created a custom program to assist clergy looking to transfer their skills to a secular employer. The program provides six months of job-prep assistance, including skills assessment, resume prep, and connection with regional job leads. At the time the initiative was launched, Dan Barker noted, "I wish there had been a service like this when I left the ministry in the 1980s. I spent a long time floundering, searching for a way to make a meaningful living as a nonbeliever. Eventually, we all have to solve the problems of life on our own, but just knowing there are resources from sympathetic organizations can be immensely helpful."

"Adam," the architect of the private forum, was the first grant recipient. In fall 2012, he sent the following message to Clergy Project members:

Finding a path out of ministry was a long journey, but I am happy to report that I am officially out of the ministry! I am now employed for a secular organization and love the freedom of not having to continue to work in ministry.

This change has been a very long time coming, over 5 years in fact, and has been the hardest thing I have ever done in my life. Juggling my deep love and commitment for my believing wife and my concern for my children's well-being with my drastically changing belief system has been quite the challenge.

Even after I started my new job, I continued to volunteer at my church until they found a replacement. Severing strong friendships of over 20 years is not something that comes easily, and in my case does not seem necessary. I remember a quote of the great Robert Ingersoll that has stuck with me from the time I changed my beliefs, that basically says, "I do not believe in martyrdom. Let those of us who can speak against religion do so and not those who are caught up in it and depend on it to support their families." (My very loose paraphrase.) In my case, I was able to internally deal with the cognitive dissonance of living a facade for so long because of the practical needs of my family. I am glad I did not go public and threaten my reputation in my community and bring unnecessary hardship on my family. Were there times I was tempted to unveil the truth? Yes, but I always sought the most reasonable option in my situation, which kept coming back to pretending to believe while I searched for other employment.

My gratitude goes out to The Clergy Project for being that oasis of sanity and reason that I needed for so long while I navigated the course that was right for me as I sought to leave the ministry. I want to recommend for those "active" clergy still out there seeking to leave the ministry that you strongly consider using the services of RiseSmart to help you hone your resume to make it attractive in the secular marketplace. I also learned several networking practices from them that helped me secure my new job.

For other "active" clergy, I also want to encourage you to hang in there. Don't give up hope. Keep searching and planning your escape, but don't bring unnecessary pain and stress into your life because you feel compelled to "tell the truth" about your changing beliefs. You owe this to no one.

Transitioning out is difficult for many reasons, but I am here to say that it can be done with no visible scars or consequences, and life is definitely better on the other side.

The generosity of Todd Stiefel and the Stiefel Freethought Foundation has made a real difference for members of the Clergy Project. On the one-year anniversary of the grant program, Todd wrote to the members of the Clergy Project, encouraging them to make use of the program:

I know many of you remain trapped behind the pulpit while secular employment eludes you. I admire your courage and your wise decision to put feeding yourself and your family ahead of the benefits of being open about your religious doubts.

A year ago, my foundation provided a grant to TCP [the Clergy Project] to start the Employment Transition Assistance Grant. This program was designed to provide "outplacement" services to members of TCP. For each grant awardee, we pay a company called RiseSmart to provide help in the job search. They provide each individual with 6 months of assistance including skills assessment, resume preparation, interview coaching, and connection with a recruiter to help you find sustainable employment. This is an approach that helps you figure out what jobs you would be good at and enjoy, and then provides direct leads to job opportunities matching your skills. Essentially, it makes you a far more marketable employment candidate.

We need your help to put it to good use. If you are able to utilize the assistance grant to find secular employment, it actually helps not just you, but also all of TCP. By having another success story, you will provide inspiration to other members that can help them through challenging times. We need you to step up and help show others examples of happy outcomes.

I know the job hunt is intimidating. You may feel you simply do not have the skills to move on to other well paying jobs. As a former executive in a large company, I think you could bring amazing experience to many careers. You folks are natural leaders. Many of you are used to managing people, finances, and even buildings. You are excellent public speakers. The reality is that you have a wide variety of highly transferable skills. Many of you have been the equivalent of CEO's in small businesses. These are skills businesses crave.

For members of the Clergy Project, leaving a career in ministry is not necessarily a direct route or even the chosen path. As you might expect, it has many ups and downs, which is why making the decision to leave ministry for a new career is particularly fraught for active clergy. Given the various competing needs and the considerable amount of risk aversion among members of the project, it makes sense for members to consider all options and flesh out a strategy, like "Adam" did, before committing to the Transitional Assistance Grant program. As will be discussed in the next chapter, one option for some, especially for those who want to be completely transparent about their beliefs but who don't want to step away from the pulpit, is to redefine "ministry" by forging new communities built around a humanist message.

10

DEVELOPING NEW COMMUNITIES

"They devoted themselves to the apostles' teaching and fellowship."
—Acts 2:42

Working with people in highly emotional situations is central to ministry. You are, for better or worse, a conduit to God, and as such are given a moral authority that is a burden. Working in ministry, you often clearly see the underlining dysfunction that faith allows to fester. It often becomes apparent that faith works against believers with its lack of transparency and its overreliance on sin, guilt, and shame. Part of being a religious person is accepting religious rules that are external to your own moral compass. As a believer, you are told that these laws will bring you freedom and that they will exalt you above worldly cares, but what is really happening is that you are being corralled. It is only after you bump into the fence that you realize your thinking is confined by prescribed rules. You do not have to look too hard for examples of this, like the Roman Catholic Church's teaching on homosexuality, its rejection of the ordination of women to the priesthood, and its ban on contraception—all "infallible" judgments that demand adherence, limit participation, and have stern punishments for failing to adhere to them.

For most members of the Clergy Project, therefore, public declaration of their loss of faith is not the crucial element of their transition. Rather, freedom comes from cutting the ties of doctrinally dependent thought and employment. This can take a variety of forms—for example, leaving ministry for an entirely new career, such as in a secular nonprofit or corporate sales, or even shifting one's existing congregation toward humanism or creating a new community based on humanism. In many cases, the desire to minister doesn't disappear after faith dissolves. In fact, for some members of the Clergy Project, the desire to do good for the sake of good takes hold, inspiring them to find a new way to serve others. A lot has been said and written about the emergence of so-called atheist churches and service groups (see the appendix). Many different organizations have emerged, such as the Sunday Assembly and the Humanist Chaplaincy at Harvard. There may be some differences in their approaches, but all are humanistic, wholly secular, and focused on community.

Mike Aus and Jerry DeWitt, both Clergy Project members, are two examples of nonbelieving clergy who continue to "minister"—without appeals to the supernatural or an all-powerful creator. To better understand this new and growing phenomenon, I conducted interviews with them to learn more about their work today as leaders of secular congregations. Jerry, through his Community Mission Chapel in Lake Charles, Louisiana, works with the Lake Charles Freethinkers to support and grow the secular community in Louisiana. One of the most well-known members of the

Clergy Project, Jerry's change in belief has not impacted his gregarious nature or optimism. He has explained in the most basic terms how his thoughts evolved in his transition from evangelical preacher to atheist: "One, God loves everybody; two, God saves everybody; three, God is in everybody; four, God is everyone's internal dialogue, and five, God is a delusion." Mike, a former Lutheran and nondenominational pastor, is now the pastor for Houston Oasis, a community of nonbelievers that articulates the following values: people are more important than beliefs; only human hands can solve human problems; reality is known through reason, not revelation; meaning comes from making a difference; labels are unimportant; and everyone should be accepted wherever they are as long as they are accepting in turn.

Jerry DeWitt

Community is something that each former clergy values, each in their own way. What impact do you think members of the Clergy Project will have on the building of secular communities?
I think that they come to the secular movement with a great deal of community-building experience. Ministers, as they go through their religious experience, naturally garner wisdom and methods and program knowledge and experience that is lacking in the secular movement. They are therefore power packed with a skill set that is instantaneously transferable to a new model re the secular community.

How has the work you do in building community changed since you lost your faith and how has it remained the same?
To be honest, it was changing already as I was moving to a more liberal theology—less of the guilt cycle, less obligation that you transferred

to the congregation in a way to encourage them to participate. It was necessary that I impose a sense of obligation when I was a conservative fundamentalist. When it comes to secular community building, we run the risk of giving birth to cats; with free will, it becomes all carrots and no sticks. I realize that the carrots are only appetizing to a certain number of people in the secular community. While I was still in ministry I was told that if I keep preaching what I am preaching I would preach myself out of a job. The obligation component is crucial within a religious context. Now, with a secular congregation the obligation to god no longer exists. Should the obligation transfer to the community? I think so. We will feel a sense of obligation in a sense of getting stuff done for the local group . . . we will adopt more of this in our community-building structures. So that we don't border on religion, I think we will be obligated to emphasize the freedom of the individual and balance this with the activism. We won't win—we will create another pseudo-religious ideology if we force conformity. We will create a similar environment. It is far trickier than with religion because there is no appeal to authority in the secular context.

What can the secular community learn about building and sustaining religion?
The secular world has to commercialize itself the same way that religion has. Because of our independence, we run the risk of artificially excluding people. Religion is always asking the question, how can I appeal to my congregation base? Religious communities have taken to caring for their members in some ways because that is good salesmanship. This process attracts people to their services. I hope that religion does this for just the right or good reasons, but honestly, this is the best method to build membership. Look at what works in the church world and access what we can mimic, such as music and sensitivity to the culture and its interests.

We need only look to groups such as the seeker-sensitive movement, which transformed church into a sort of religious mall. From my perspective as a fundamentalist, this model was the antichrist, this was all salesmanship; there was no spirituality. But even I couldn't deny that these services were successful, having congregations of 15,000 to 20,000.

So, what makes these megachurches so successful? Well, first, we need to acknowledge that they are securing engagement. There is something going on every night of the week. Programs are created and tailored to service the needs of the people coming to the community.

In my opinion, churches are spiritual business, so when it comes to creating incentives, we in the secular community can run into a problem in trying to replicate churches. Even for churches, this is a challenge as they may seem insincere. When it comes to the secular community, we need to make sure our motives are transparent.

Another big thing is the emotional side of religion; we need to acknowledge, and on some level embrace, emotion. Religion enjoys emotion and at times exploits it. The secular community tends to fear this experience. One of the ways that we are vulnerable is when we take polarizing positions, and in some ways, this allows us to be lazy, even intellectually lazy. The hardest thing would be to balance the emotional needs of the people looking for secular community with the desire to be firmly rooted in reason and intellect. When you're building community it takes commitment from everyone in it. With religion it is easier to do this when everyone is repeating the same ideology; in secular community the challenge arrives in divergence. Though independent thought is idealized, it has to be balanced with the common goal.

Another thing to keep in mind is that modern-day Christians are not necessarily giving out of fear or guilt. They want to be recognized for what they are doing. Specifically, they want the pastor to notice what they are doing. I can't tell you how many times I've seen people who instead of putting their tithe in the plate put it in the pastor's hand, so he knows their contribution, just in case writing your name on the envelope is not enough. The closest we have in the secular community is buying a book by Richard Dawkins and asking him to sign it.

There are so many pieces in the religious congregation model. The idea of a fan base or cult of personality seems like a coercive mechanism, but in reality, it actually functions. It is a cog in the communal wheel that allows others to work around it. Community in my experience never floats without a leader; the leader does make a difference.

Mike Aus

Community is something that each former clergy values, each in their own way. What impact do you think members of the Clergy Project will have on the building of secular communities?
Focusing totally on Houston Oasis, it takes a full-time commitment to make a community come together, marketing team, youth team; pieces are coming together for building an institution of influence. We started with less than twenty people and are now averaging a hundred people a week. People are getting a vision of what it takes to build something of significance. The thing about the freethought movement is that no one bothered to build an institution. If we could build a secular institution that was focused on community, it could stand against the institutional influence of religions.

But we can't make a community happen without the investment of time and resources. I always say, freethought isn't free. It costs a lot for people to volunteer their time. I have been thinking about building community differently than I had previously, specifically, from a marketing standpoint. I have become more and more convinced that the term "atheist" is toxic—25 percent of Americans are "nones" but only 3 percent are willing to call themselves atheists. I think we need to find a way to touch people. Facts don't give us passion, they are not encouraging. A focus on the affect is lacking from the atheist movement by and large.

I am convinced that the growth of the freethought movement will come from the people sitting in pews right now; I think this is where the wave will come from. Large atheist organizations have limited donors and contributors. This is not a movement when you compare it to the numbers that are currently sitting in pews—people who up until this point have not identified as atheist.

How has the work you do building community changed since you lost your faith and how has it remained the same?

Well, there are a lot of differences and similarities. I would say that the similarities lie in bringing people together and caring for one another. A good community builder can nurture those relationships. The real difference working with freethinkers is you tend to have people in the community who are more focused on the vision, mission, and values. Unlike in religious communities, where they have mystical religious interpretations or fuzzy questions such as, what would Jesus want us to do? In humanist communities, people are committed to reason and to a thoughtful decision-making process. Because of this, I think that there is the potential for secular humanist communities to be healthier, but we still need to have adherence to core or common values. There needs to be some factors that engender cohesiveness. In the case of Houston Oasis, our core values are listed on our Web site. Also, adherence to this new creed is a choice not a fear. We are guided by core values, which define our community, and they shape our interactions with each other, society, and the world.

What do you think the secular community can learn from churches?

First, I have to say it is a huge mistake for people in the freethought community to denigrate religious institutions. They have been around longer than any others and we have to learn from that. I was thrilled when one of our members came across Rick Warren's The Purpose Driven Church. It is one of the best books I've ever read about building community. People might not agree, but I think we can learn stuff from this guy. I mean tell me how you can build a congregation with 20,000 in attendance? For we humanists the exciting part is that we are free of the religion garbage, but we can master the institutional side of it, harnessing the power of small groups, building an infrastructure that services the community's needs. Freethinkers enjoy hospital visits as much as religious people! Pastoral care, the secular community could use an element of that; it is crucial to engagement.

I have been trying to let it grow organically, but really what we are doing is providing opportunities to build relationships; this is something that is going to take decades to see it grow.

To grow membership from the so-called nones, we need to keep in mind that you win influence by offering a better alternative, not by belittling others. Have a series of potluck suppers, in different areas of the city, to provide opportunities for people to get to know each other. Family friendly happy hour! A chance to bring families together, providing opportunities so that community supports are cultivated. How many faces do you see repeated through all the [national secular] events? What that tells me is they are getting their need for community filled by doing the rounds of conventions. Why can't we make this happen every week in every community in America? Human beings need a community where they can find babysitters for their kids, find friends, hear about business deals, and connect. Not everyone can afford to go to conventions, but they can participate in secular communities locally.

11

CONFRONTING LOSSES

*"For in much wisdom is much vexation,
and those who increase knowledge increase sorrow."*
—Ecclesiastes 1:18

Since joining the Clergy Project, I have heard it said more than once that losing faith is not a loss but a gain. No longer being concerned with a vengeful "peeping Tom" deity, or Bronze and Iron Age social mores that have long outlived their usefulness, allows for a newfound sense of post-theistic freedom. Despite the histrionics on the part of believers, this freedom does not include uncontrolled evil and debauchery, but rather a quiet acceptance of our insignificance and the awe-inspiring reality of seeing life as it truly is, unfettered by wish-fulfilling notions and superstition. Still, for nonbelieving clergy, the feeling of isolation can be utterly alienating. The psychological, social, and familial aspects of disbelief in many ways dwarf the potential financial implications. After I left seminary, I spent many hours wondering why I seemed to be the only seminary grad that had rejected her religious tradition. I even felt some residual Catholic guilt and shame in accepting that I was no longer a theist. I was happy to be free of the Church, but I still lived in fear of what might happen if family or friends discovered my atheism. Similarly, the isolated existence of closeted clergy members could be likened to finding yourself adrift in a fog on the Pacific. It is not long before you will see the world as a very alienating place. The Clergy Project has helped temper this sense of isolation by throwing a lifeline. Even so, for many, the true loss is not faith itself, but rather, the often-associated loss of relationships—and the inevitable loss of one's old self-identity.

I have thought quite a lot about the concept of shunning in religious families. It is something that lay at the back of my mind throughout my journey, a consequence that I knew I would eventually have to face when my mother discovered the Clergy Project. I knew that the stakes would be high, that the influence of my mother's religious beliefs would ultimately adversely affect our relationship.

On many occasions over the past decade, I have spoken briefly with my mother about my lack of faith and my atheism. Though I never lied to her, I did attempt to downplay my secular activism. I wanted to ensure some measure of transparency and truth telling in our relationship, but also to limit the details and frequency of these conversations, so that we could carve out space where our relationship could thrive. It was, I had thought, a happy but uncomfortable truce. Unfortunately, this strategy came crashing down in 2013, just before my birthday.

One thing you should know about my mother is that she is a deeply religious person—her adherence to Roman

Catholic orthodoxy is consistent, her faith unshakeable, and her demand for capitulation absolute. Growing up in her Catholic home was an exercise in extreme limits. The *scala naturea*, or "great chain of being," dictated that my parents—in particular, my mother—had absolute authority over me. The only authority to which she submitted was that of the Church and of God.

As a child, I did not know that praying the rosary on my knees every night was an out-of-the-ordinary event, that saying novenas was not a spare-time activity, and that other children did not feel shame and guilt for the crucifixion and death of Jesus. In all respects, I was an indoctrinated child. I can remember the feel of the pink-glass rosary beads between my fingers; the repetitive nature of the call and response prayer was calming. The rosary came from France. It had a pewter centerpiece and a glass dome, from which water from the Lourdes Shrine had long-since evaporated. The crucifix and chain links were well worn; between the first and second decades, one link became loose, and the rosary would often come apart as I clutched the beads in my hands, intently in prayer. My mind and heart were focused on contrition as I sought the calming presence of the hand of God with each repeated Hail Mary. *"Holy Mary, mother of God, pray for us sinners, now and at the hour of our death. Amen."*

I called upon the Holy Mother to intercede on my behalf, despite my unworthiness, and I knew that the only salvation for my sinfulness was penitence. Sadly, this pattern of extreme religious adherence plagued me until I went to college and began studying theology. Slowly, reason began to infiltrate the medieval worldview in which I had been raised. Life on the outside was at once thought provoking, exciting, and terrifying. My transformation from theist to atheist took many years and incarnations, but a constant threat to my personal development and intellectual growth was fear of my mother's judgment and criticism.

Despite all of this, I confronted the fear honestly and, before I completed my master's degree, told my mother that I was no longer a believer in God. Given the limited discussion on this topic over the years, I had thought her silence was an expression of her commitment to our relationship. Sadly, I now think that she had been waiting for the right time to confront me. The day before my birthday, my mother took me to dinner, just the two of us. I had expected an easygoing conversation about getting older and life changes. But almost immediately, right after we ordered, she jumped to a discussion of morality. I attempted to distract her and downplay her adversarial tone, but these attempts failed as she sternly focused on my liberal transgressions and my rejection of Catholic orthodoxy. It quickly became apparent that she was very angry and that she had discussed my apostasy with someone else, most likely a priest. In her opinion, I had not received the "right kind of theological training" and my loss of faith was the fault of my educators. I attempted to dissuade her from this conversation, to make light of it and move on, but she could not let it go.

My ideas and values were contrary to Catholicism and thus wrong. Her critique went on. According to her, I was immoral, decrepit, and godless. The worst transgression, in her opinion, was that my actions were an affront to her status, and I owed her the decency of capitulating. I attempted to appease her without compromising my integrity, but unfortunately, she interpreted this as a continuation of my "abhorrent and disrespectful behavior." I tried again at length to negotiate common ground, but after being confronted by continually escalating histrionics, in which she characterized me as "the devil," "ungrateful," and "disrespectful," and my husband and I as "immoral perverts," I recognized the cold fact: her faith was more important to her than our relationship.

Unfortunately, I am not the only member of the Clergy Project or the wider atheist community who has experienced this kind of negative reaction from a family member regarding their nonbelief. The potential impact on personal relationships is one of the biggest deterrents for Clergy Project members who are thinking about coming out as an atheist. It is naive to underestimate the motivation that one feels to sustain primary relationships. It is a sad testament to the power of religious indoctrination that some believers will sacrifice relationships because they are unwilling or unable to recognize that a change in belief has not irrevocably altered the person they love.

For Clergy Project members and for atheists who have struggled with religious family members, the sting of shunning may remain, but the ability to cope can be buttressed by the support of a community of peers. I now recognize that my mother perceives me as an outsider and that this perception, however artificial, delineates a clear end to our relationship. Nothing I can say to her will change these facts. Moving forward, I can only mourn, accept, and refuse to allow religious dysfunction to infiltrate my gratitude for my life, for my husband and son, and for my community.

Losing relationships is not the only loss that members of the project detail after leaving their faith. For most of us, faith played a significant role in our lives and in how we understood and defined ourselves. Faith was more than an idea or talisman that we held close to our hearts; it had a life of its own, it was imbued with power and deemed essential to survival. I had an opportunity to speak at length about the losses associated with rejecting one's faith with Mary Johnson, a former nun who served in the Missionaries of Charity. I had read her memoir, *An Unquenchable Thirst*, in which she details her twenty-year journey as a sister and her work with Mother Teresa. Reading her words, I found myself laughing and weeping in remembrance of the believer I had been, and in recognition of the humanist I have become. I told Mary that her book had led me to consider, for the first time since leaving Catholicism, the things that I had lost when I left my faith. We began to reminisce about our former lives and identities, listing off the many things that we have left behind, including rites and rituals that we had enjoyed. One of the things high on that list, believe it or not, was prayer. Mostly this was due to the fact that prayer provided the space for silence, and that silence is something that is not necessarily cultivated in the secular world. At one point during this conversation, I looked at Mary and said, "This well that we drank from is too deep."

Losing faith is not something that Clergy Project members set out to do when they first started asking questions about their beliefs. In fact, many would say that their search for answers represented an attempt to better understand their faith and to have more impact as a religious leader and person of faith. But once you are confronted by the uncomfortable glare of your own reasoned assessment, there is little left to cling to as you face the loneliness of your loss of faith. As members of the Clergy Project, our religious lives took years to construct; they are part of our formation and our history. We may have extracted our beliefs, but we cannot extract their imprint on our lives. In many ways, our past experiences have made us who we are, and we are challenged to take what we have learned and reanimate our values in light of reason and the beauty of reality. We have learned that despite the losses, outside the walls of faith, the truth is beautiful.

12

LOOKING AHEAD

"Know that wisdom is such to your soul; if you find it,
you will find a future, and your hope will not be cut off."
—Proverbs 24:14

My transition from a person of faith to a person of reason was not a short or thoughtless journey. As with other Clergy Project members, it took into account not only my theological training, but also the fabric of my culture and the expectations of my family. A seminary education creates a chasm, like that of a glacial drift from which clergy must either cross or evade. The Christianity that I was introduced to in my studies bore limited similarities to the religious and spiritual ideology that I, and other Clergy Project members, endorsed as believers. The theological precipice from which believing clergy may find themselves dangling should not be feared. As many members of the Clergy Project can attest, letting go of god and all things supernatural can be an extremely liberating experience—one that, though mired with challenges, brings with it a fresh vision of the world and its beauty.

I do not tend to spend much time in churches these days. It is not that I am consciously avoiding them; it's just that they no longer come up as places to go. I think it is like that for a lot of people now. My need for religious community has moved on. The long, slow decline of religion has been pushed beyond its boundaries into the oncoming surge of science, technology, globalism, and universal rights. The insular, tribal, and small world in which I was raised has evaporated, and today the world is a much bigger place for me.

For the individual, this journey out of faith is not a straight path. For society as a whole, these individual journeys comprise a quiet revolution whose results are showing themselves in the rise of the "nones"—those who attest no religious affiliation—which, according to the 2014 General Social Survey, today account for 21 percent of the U.S. population. This figure is especially striking when considering that, until the 1990s, this figure sat under 10 percent for decade upon decade. Assuming this upward trend continues—and there is no reason to think it won't—"nones" will soon represent a larger demographic in the United States than Catholics, which currently represent 24 percent of the population.

The Clergy Project is part of this zeitgeist, a virtual sanctuary where those who have shed the dogma of their splintering religious traditions can emerge autonomously and anonymously online. To extend the conversation about shedding faith and the role that doubt plays in belief beyond the boundaries of the Clergy Project's members-only forum, Linda LaScola and I host the blog Rational Doubt (www. patheos.com/blogs/rationaldoubt/) on Patheos, a multifaith Web platform. The aim of this blog, which features members of the Clergy Project as guest contributors, is to encourage input from the outside, including religious leaders and believers, on subjects such as humanism, biblical scholarship, and life after religion. It also aims to make the issues surrounding loss of faith more tangible and accessible to the broader public and to encourage thoughtful dialogue and active listening.

It is a long, arduous process to untangle oneself from the influence of religious ideology, particularly when you are a perpetrator of said ideology. I spent many years tilling the eroding soil of my faith, like a farmer trying to save her fields from being taken by the sea. For a while I was even smugly satisfied that my faith was protected as I squirreled away my doubts. I did not want to leave the Church. But in the end, the evidence against the truth of Catholicism kept mounting, and the Church kept ignoring its culpability in manipulating and harming its followers. Eventually I could no longer contain the flood of doubt and disdain in which I was awash. The role of the Clergy Project in providing peer support is a crucial step in dismantling the mystique of faith and religion—a beginning place on a journey away from belief-based decisions and toward reasoned deliberation.

We have the privilege of living in a time when information can be easily and readily shared. Whether we are cognizant of it or not, the ease and speed by which we communicate is as important, if not more important, than the messages we are sharing. When it comes to the decline of religion, many contributing factors are emerging. The Clergy Project is just one of many branches in a new tree, nourished by the bright lights of science and reason and humanist values, that will soon overshadow religion. Given that we are on the cusp of this transition, it is difficult to assert with absolute authority that this new growth will completely replace wilting religious ideologies, but it is without doubt that religion today faces a challenge that it has never before faced, especially in the West. Initiatives like the Clergy Project aside, a number of other factors are contributing to the decline of religion.

Education is a great equalizer, and with it, individuals attain not only status in society, but also the ability to internalize status and use this to communicate their values and to have these values reflected back to them by their wider community. With the expansion of education and the sharing of knowledge, first through the Cathedral schools and universities and now through multiple forms of media, we see an improvement in basic knowledge of science, history, mathematics, and philosophy. This expansion of education calls into question the previously stated "truths" that religions have used to fill the gaps in knowledge. Now that social media and the Internet have become a dominant player in information sharing, the only arena left to religious truths is that of willful ignorance or cognitive dissonance.

Corruption is also a major factor contributing to the decline of religion. The Catholic Church immediately springs to mind as a prime example of corruption in action. For many believers, hypocrisy and corruption have erected a roadblock directly in front of the church door. This hypocrisy is not isolated to Catholicism, but in this example, we see the mightiest fall. Despite the privileged status that religious organizations have, money and impropriety are a consistent reality. One only needs to look at the often opulent surroundings of clergy to see where donations end up.

Assisting with this erosion of faith is the repudiation of so-called traditional or conservative values in favor of universal rights. Secular communities like the Clergy Project are sitting on the vanguard of this new values system. Being on the cutting edge is a pretty exciting place to be, but my hope is that one day there will be no need for an initiatives like the Clergy Project—or for an atheist movement. Specifically, I hope for a future where religion, if it is still practiced, is a benign personal preference—a future where religious communities and humanist communities happily coexist, embracing and expanding the concept of multifaith to include ethical values and thereby acknowledging similarities rather than differences. It is my long-held hope that religious leaders will speak honestly with their congregations about the nature of what is taught in seminary, and communicate this "secret knowledge" in place of sermons based on long-expired ideologies and a senescent interpretation of scripture.

Atheism is not an ideology, but a conclusion that utilizes an epistemology of reason. As such, atheists look not to popes or holy men but to facts. Though the atheist movement has leaders, they are not idols to be worshipped or toppled from their pedestals. Rather, they are lightning rods, drawing attention to our secular position while encouraging dialogue and articulating our shared values. That said, I am not so naive to believe that lower levels of religiosity and fewer appeals to faith will solve all the world's ills or offer a panacea. Atheists, humanists, and freethinkers may have seen through religion, but we are still susceptible to the fallacies and faults that characterize all human beings. Linda LaScola offers a cautionary mantra that sums up this fact: "atheists are people too." I think we would all do well to keep that in mind as we engage with one another, and with the wider public.

This journey from our ancient past, as ancestor worshippers, to polytheists, to monotheists, has not proven to be a smooth transition, but it is one with an obvious trajectory. In the not-too-distant future, the secular movement will surge to a critical mass, decreasing the need for its message—a large task but one that is already under way. For now, the reality for Clergy Project members is this: though we are apostates who have rejected faith and the supremacy of sacred literature to control our lives and dictate our growing and expanding value systems, we remain the same people who committed our lives to the values of compassion, ethics, and empathy.

As members of the Clergy Project, we have lived on both sides of the fence; we have tasted the power of belief and have rejected it as an illusion. I, like most members of the project, am glad that I have shed my faith and happy that we have been welcomed and encouraged by the secular community. Richard Dawkins, Dan Barker, Daniel Dennett, Linda LaScola, and all who helped launch the project and raise awareness about nonbelieving clergy have given us an invaluable resource. Now that the forum is tested and proven, and continues to grow and morph, we are finally able to ask, what will be our contribution as a whole to the deinstitutionalization of religion?

As active and former clergy, we keep witness to the chaos that is the world, influenced by competing religiosity and ego-ridden spirituality. Getting away from a world overrun by theocratic tendencies to a harmonious humanist utopia is not a one-step process. It will take more than just removing religion from the altar of authority it now claims; it will require people and communities committed to humanism to make that happen—communities like the Clergy Project.

For me, the Clergy Project is the incarnation of social change. Together, the varied voices and cultural experiences of its members rattle the very foundations of religion. Unified, our voices erode theocratic supremacy, poking holes in its hollow dogma. We seek freedom from the fragmented religious adolescence that has so far hindered humanity's ability to grasp hold of reality and hope to contribute to making the world a better place in the here and now. In some ways, it is ironic that a closeted, private group like the Clergy Project could have so much potential to influence the future of religion. This does not mean that members of the project wish to utterly eradicate religion. Rather, they hope that it continues to decline, that theism's outdated worldview is put aside like other childish things, and that humanism thrives in its place.

Humanism—in the simplest terms, being good without god, or being good for goodness' sake—is the answer to the question that humanity has been asking since the spark of imagination first erupted in our ancestors' brains. Atheism is not just the rejection of god. It reflects an openness to reality and a willingness to honestly follow evidence where it leads. These traits—and not blind faith—are what should be communicated and transmitted to future generations.

As former clergy who have left churches of every denomination, synagogues, mosques, convents, monasteries, and theological institutions, we stand as examples of the reasonableness of doubt and its thoughtful conclusions. I cannot help but think that we offer a compelling voice for why science and secularism do a better job than religion and superstition of answering the so-called ultimate questions. If my story and those that I have shared can attest to anything, it is that this debate is long from dead. We apostates, who have fled a religious worldview, have come to see that though secularism and science are not necessarily warm and fuzzy, they do provide answers that are verifiable and truthful—and in the words of Richard Dawkins, the "truth is beautiful."

EPILOGUE

"Peace be to you; do not fear."
—Judges 6:23

This book began with comments regarding doubt. It seems only fitting that it end with a few final thoughts on the subject.

Any clergy, whether believing or not, would say that doubt is a constant companion for all believers. For those doubters reading this book, I empathize with your lonely struggle. I understand the constant and subtle discomfort that lurks in your thoughts—and the lonely, scary, and continual process of trying to reestablish your connection with the divine. Knowledge helped me break this cycle. It can help you too.

When you are reared to think of your faith and its leaders as infallible, dissent can be an unsettling thing. This is particularly true for clergy, who have devoted their lives to the subject of faith. I therefore especially hope that this story reaches those clergy who have yet to articulate their doubts. As they struggle through this process, I am thankful that they can look to the Clergy Project as an example of community and humanism as an example of good.

APPENDIX

In my role as acting executive director of the Clergy Project, I asked Linda LaScola and her colleague, Pamela Blake, if they would complete a preliminary study of four emerging secular congregations. They provided me with the following sketches of these humanist communities in June 2013.

HOUSTON OASIS
Thumbnail
- Former Lutheran minister, male, age 48
- Came out publicly as an atheist on television, in the spring of 2012
- Was approached by former members of his congregation to start a humanist community
- Spearheaded by dedicated 12-person committee
- Community is up and running as of September 2012
- Weekly Sunday 10:30 a.m. gatherings of 70 to 100+ people
- Monthly discussion/support group, "Transition to Reason"
- Smart Recovery group, a secular alternative to 12-step program
- Children's education program and child care

- Blood drive, quarterly
- Timeline: 3 months from start to launch
- Leadership structure: eight member board; former minister serves as ex-officio board member with title of executive director

What worked in setting it up
- Dedicated committee of generous and talented volunteers with diverse skills
- Being aligned around a clear vision; creating core value statements from scratch
- Large single donations of meeting space and sound system
- Good relationships with local freethought groups to establish credibility
- 501(c)3 status is "huge ... says we're in it for the long haul"
- Publicity via word of mouth, social media, Web site, print media, and YouTube channel
- Creating community and meaning
- Bylaws modeled on nonprofit samples found on Secretary of State Web site

Greatest challenges in setting it up
- Lack of seed money up front
- Insufficient publicity leading up to launch
- Limited funds
- Finding a suitable location

What makes gatherings successful
- Meet weekly on Sunday mornings (10:30 a.m. to noon), when most people are available
- Live music is key—large pool of local talent; use rotating

musicians who work for $100 or donate their time
- Presentations with thought-provoking, compelling messages
- High-profile guest speakers/tie-ins with other community organizations
- Extended coffee hour and meet & greet
- Fellowship; "come early, stay late"; optional lunch afterward in local restaurant

Short-term goals
- Hire full salaried staff
- Develop youth program
- Improve financial position; anticipate increased income due to recent 501(c)3 status; address issue of whether to institute pledge policy
- Evolve naturally to expand human services and grow the community
- Create "Free Thought Center"—free books, coffee bar for discussions, counselors on staff

Longer-term goals
- Expand to satellite locations in metropolitan area
- Create "megachurch"; expand movement to other states
- Contribute to creation of larger atheist community with hundreds of thousands of members around the country

Advice to others
- Start with sufficient funds—$10,000 minimum
- Assemble a team of gifted, capable, outgoing people who are committed to a shared vision; maximum 12 people
- Focus on networking—"increases chances of success exponentially"

- Apply for and obtain 501(c)3 designation
- Be clear about what your mission is
- If you have any doubt, don't do it

Mission statement and core beliefs
A community grounded in reason, celebrating the human experience
- *People are more important than beliefs*
- *Only human hands can solve human problems*
- *Reality is known through reason, not revelation*
- *Meaning comes from making a difference*
- *Labels are unimportant*
- *Everyone should be accepted wherever they are as long as they are accepting in return*

C3 EXCHANGE
Thumbnail
- Former Anglican Minister, male, age 45
- Hand selected by bishop and tasked with leading a Reformed Church of America through its evolution to a humanist community
- Timeline: 7 years since transition began
- At onset, 400 attendance; currently, 200 attendance
- Implemented changes consistent with humanist ethos, including changing name and removing cross from building; programs focus on justice issues and the five Ancient Greek values (individualism, rationalism, justice, beauty, the pursuit of excellence), with thin ties to tradition
- Transition is ongoing—currently "on fuzzy ground whether a church or not . . . the experiment continues"
- Leadership structure: 12-member board; formerly led by elders

What worked in setting it up

- Taking recognizable steps to move past identity of church; having a conversation about changes before they occurred
- Free publicity from Fox News, when they created controversy around removing the cross
- Having core group of church members who were in habit of giving time and money to organization and who understood what it takes to run a church-like organization
- Being authentic and being "out there" in the community; participating in debates, taking a stand on issues, letters to editor, volunteerism
- Having structure of church organization in place for pledges and endowments; having staff in place; having offices and physical place to meet

Greatest challenges in setting it up

- No template; no external support; no peers
- Managing change and its impact on the community; finding balance between retaining what is comfortable to current members and making changes that help community evolve
- Church members resistant to change; upheaval created by dissent and loss of long-term members
- Mortgage debt levels too high; members attached to church building; building was too churchy

What makes gatherings successful

- Compelling speaker; meaningful and relevant messages
- Live music; music as part of change
- Sunday mornings have three parts: small groups, main gathering, and talk back
- Connections; shared values; creating community

Short-term goals
- Continue going forward and "rounding out the edges"; build community; continue to evolve

Longer-term goals
- Take leadership role beyond the community; establish a group or be part of a group that makes humanist communities repeatable and sustainable
- Work toward vision of a loose confederation of groups/umbrella group/franchise model to support humanist communities by:
    - Agreeing to shared universal principles
    - Providing pool of trained leaders and communities for leaders to go to
    - Providing practical resources—programming, governance, finances, retirement funds, children's programs, continuation schemes, technology—the kinds of things that denominations offer
    - Convening conferences to provide connections with other communities/regions/nations and to boost morale and combat isolation
    - Sharing speakers
    - Providing tie-ins with universities; creating career paths for students

Advice to others
- "Get a clear vision and go for it"
- Have a compelling leader who can bring a team around him/herself and be authentic
- Partner with people who share the vision and are compelling, can organize, value the arts, can bring best business practices
- Connect with like-minded groups

- Music is important
- Need courage to keep going

Mission statement and core beliefs
C3 Exchange, a pioneer in the Inclusive Spiritual Movement, offers resources to enrich and empower the lives of all people in body, mind, and spirit. C3 Exchange follows these core values:

- *Pursuing Inclusive Spirituality—We value the inclusive spiritual journey. We welcome people of all faiths and no faith. All people are encouraged to craft their individual spiritual journey in a safe, supportive community.*
- *Pursuing Activism—We seek to be the change we wish to see in the world. Liberation begins as an inner freedom that inspires liberation in others. We value community collaborations and global partnerships, ensuring that life, liberty, and the pursuit of happiness are honored for ALL.*
- *Pursuing Sustainability—We seek a future in harmony with the earth. We value the earth as "God's Body." We are part of the earth and therefore our fate and the earth's fate are entwined. We seek to live in tune with nature's patterns, educate ourselves about earth's resources, and seek a future where we live in harmony with the earth.*
- *Pursuing Wellness—We value holistic health as an expression of "spiritual" or integral well-being. We see nutrition, emotional health, yoga, relationships, and spiritual practice such as prayer and meditation as being core components of health.*
- *Celebrating Gender—We value gender complementarities. Gender difference is an expression of the diversity that is built into nature. We follow in a long tradition of celebrating "Goddess" as the creative impulse, and "Gaia"*

as the feminine energy of flow and interrelatedness. In practical terms, we intentionally honor women's journeys as well as men's journeys; we value storytelling and group dynamics, yin and yang compassion, active and receptive modes of community.

- *Celebrating Sexuality—Sexuality is an expression of our humanity, and all sexuality is to be affirmed. We are an open and affirming community. We value the "coming out" journey of all people and seek to create a safe environment to support each other in this process.*

- *Celebrating Inquiry—As life evolves, so do beliefs and values. We follow no particular doctrine or orthodoxy. We encourage independent thinking. We celebrate all minds and all disciplines, the interplay of religion and science, sociology and spirituality, psychology and religious tradition. Together, we explore tangible, daily life issues such as work, ethics, relationships, and health with searching questions and open curiosity.*

- *Celebrating Creativity—We value the arts, as creative expression of the deepest human yearnings. We honor the mystery of Life, and the manifestation of this mystery includes and transcends words, in diverse artistic expression.*

- *Celebrating Interspirituality—We celebrate universal truths. We celebrate diversity of religious and wisdom perspective. Our community is made up of people identifying as Christian, Jew, Muslim, Hindu, Buddhist, humanist, and no particular identification. While our primary language and story are referenced from Christianity, we celebrate the universal truths that come through all traditions. We value interfaith dialogue as a movement for a more peaceful world.*

- *Celebrating Community—We value community where*

compassion and interrelatedness are expressions of the unity of life. Participation isn't so much about beliefs and rituals as it is about learning to be human together. We value our local community, the global community of which we are a part, and the web of life that sustains us and depends on our care.

WEST HILL UNITED CHURCH OF CANADA

Thumbnail

- United Church of Canada minister, female, age 54
- Has written two books on progressive Christianity themes
- Determined that people's elementary beliefs were being reinforced by the Christian liturgy despite the academic approach they heard (if listening) in the sermons
- Told her congregation in a sermon that she did not think God was listening, that there was no God
- Board familiar with concepts of liberal Christianity supported her in making changes.
- Won an 11 to 4 vote on a heresy hearing
- Initiated a transition from Christian to humanist community, staying within United Church of Canada system
- Lost 40 percent of original community (from 40 to 29 families), those who were not ready to make such drastic changes (e.g., taking Lord's Prayer out of the service and not promising eternal life)
- Stopped using the word "God" because it was so vague as to be misleading
- Leadership structure: 11-member board that "makes decisions on policies, processes, and issues relevant to congregational life"

What worked in setting it up
- Strong board support, even as members were shifting in and out
- Support within the congregation
- Introduction of critical inquiry, study groups focusing on liberal Christian authors
- The document that members wrote together in 2009 focusing on how they wanted to live

Greatest challenges in setting it up
- Turnover of church members
- Not receiving active support of the national church, which chose to focus on supporting churches with more conservative immigrant members

What makes gatherings successful
- Meet weekly on Sunday mornings at 10:30 a.m.
- Good music provided by staff musicians
- Variety of sermon topics, not scripture centered
- Guest speakers from secular and progressive Christian communities
- After-service refreshments, bringing the time spent together on Sunday morning to about two hours
- "Visitors and travelers lunch" the first Sunday of the month, especially for people who have come from long distances

Short-term goals
- Maintain and grow membership
- Continue successful programs
- Focus on social justice instead of saving souls

Longer-term goals
- Identify the nature of the work the congregation wants to do—what are the people's needs that the community is fulfilling?
- Engage in a dialogue about how to live out the community's values
- Provide assistance to other emerging humanist communities

Advice to others
- If transitioning a Christian congregation, try to gauge member openness to change before making major changes
- Assemble and keep a good board of directors
- Develop a clear mission with broad community input
- Be ready for conflict and setbacks

Mission statement and core beliefs
Moved by a reverence for life to pursue justice for all, we inspire one another to seek truth, live fully, care deeply, and make a difference.

SUNDAY ASSEMBLY
Thumbnail
- Started by two (M/F) stand-up comedians in the UK in their early 30s
- One is a former advertising salesman who had done "community-based" comedy shows in which he personally sold tickets to people at the door. Had thought about the concept of a church for nonbelievers for about six years. His idea was rejuvenated when discussing it with the other comedian founder who also liked the idea.
- Both have Anglican backgrounds. She attended lively Pentecostal services with friends as a teenager. His church

involvement dropped off when his mother died when he was young.

- First service, which was preceded by much press attention, was held in early 2013 in a rented abandoned church
- Now holding two sessions on every first Sunday of the month

What worked in setting it up
- Use of social and traditional media—reaching out; receiving a lot of free publicity
- Billing it as "part foot-stomping show, part atheist church"
- Forming an advisory group of regular attendees who have business expertise
- Applying business and advertising principles to attract attendees and develop an appealing service and practices that can be exported to other communities

Greatest challenges in setting it up
- Still a work in progress—the next challenge will be to grow the model to other areas, in the UK and abroad.

What makes gathering successful
- Having two sessions per Sunday (after the huge success of the initial services)
- Rousing music and a different theme each week, but with the same order of service, including singing popular songs, reflection, and a talk, often by a visiting speaker
- Interesting, humorous talks
- Refreshments afterward in the church
- Some people meeting later in a nearby pub

Short-term goals
- Maintain and grow membership
- Continue successful programs
- Focus on community engagement
- Focus on enjoying this life

Longer-term goals
- Get a better sense of the demographics and interests of the people who attend
- Become more formally involved in worthwhile community activities
- Provide a framework for groups in other locations to start up their own operation
- Become financially viable via attendee donations and fees from growing groups in other locales
- Continue to focus on community engagement and enjoying this life

Advice to others
- Advice at this point is mainly in the form of helping others set up "branches" or "franchises" (for lack of better terms). An engaging leader is paramount in attracting and keeping attendees.

Mission statement and core beliefs
- *Live better, help often; wonder more.*
- *The goal is to solace worries, provoke kindness and inject a bit more whizziness into the everyday*

ACKNOWLEDGMENTS

This book, which tells my story as a clergy member who lost her faith and the Clergy Project's short history as a community, is also a thank you to the project's founders. With their one simple act, they have forever influenced my life and the lives of other Clergy Project members. I therefore would like to extend special thanks to each of them:

Dan Barker, who generously gave me the title for this book, *From Apostle to Apostate.* As a project founder and member, Dan has been a great supporter, both while I wrote this book and during my time as acting executive director. I would also like to thank his copresident at the Freedom From Religion Foundation and wife, *Annie Laurie Gaylor,* for her support of the Clergy Project.

Robin Elisabeth Cornwell, who has gone to bat for the Clergy Project and for me many, many times. She is a mentor, and a friend whose compassion and commitment is an inspiration.

Richard Dawkins, who is not only a founder but also a sustainer of the Clergy Project, with the Richard Dawkins Foundation for Reason and Science funding the project since its inception. He has acted without seeking fanfare or praise, and his ongoing support speaks to his generous nature and kind heart.

Dan Dennett, to whom I owe a debt for responding to my initial e-mail and for his ongoing support. His genuine concern for faithless clergy, evident in his coauthored studies "Preachers Who Are Not Believers" and *Caught in the Pulpit*, is moving

Linda LaScola, whom I first knew as a researcher working with Dan Dennett, has become a colleague and a friend. Our first efforts were with the Clergy Project and we now work together on the Rational Doubt blog. Thank you, Linda, I would not want to do this work with anyone else.

To *Adam*, the architect of the private forum and friend, your leadership motivated me to do what I can to help my Clergy Project "brothers and sisters." When I emerged on the forum, you made me feel so welcomed! *Chris*, I am so grateful for the work you did in helping set up the project. Your kindness and support embody the meaning of friendship and the reciprocity and altruism of this community. Thank you to you both for the work that you did to make the project happen. At the time that the forum launched, you were both in active ministry. Know that much of the work that I did as acting executive director was to help you and the other "actives." I am thankful for the opportunity to do what I can to make a difference.

I would also like to extend special thanks to those Clergy Project members who assisted me with this book and with my own personal growth. *Jerry DeWitt*, thank you for the hours of conversation and your insights into secular communities—

you will always be my "brother." *Mike Aus*, you broke down many barriers when you came out, more so when you began Houston Oasis. My thanks to you both for your leadership. I look forward to seeing what you will do next. *Tom Rastrelli*, thank you for allowing me to share your story, and for your support and friendship. I am so grateful to call you a friend. *Mary Johnson*, my "sister," there are so many common threads in our narratives. I am very thankful that I count you as a friend. *Robert Parham*, thank you for allowing me to share your story, and for all your efforts on behalf of the Clergy Project. To all the other members of the Clergy Project, and to those closeted and doubting clergy, may you find a place to speak truth and revel in the reality that you are not alone.

I would like to acknowledge Pitchstone and *Kurt Volkan*, who gave me the opportunity to tell the story of the Clergy Project and my experience of losing faith.

Finally and most importantly, I must thank my husband and my son, whose love and support has encouraged and fortified me throughout the writing of this book. I love you, and I hope in reading this book you come to understand that without you both, I could not have completed the task of telling this story.

NOTES

All quoted biblical passages come from the *HarperCollins Study Bible: New Revised Standard Version.*

Prologue
The Clery Project's stated mission is to "provide educational, charitable, and peer support to current and former religious professionals who no longer hold supernatural beliefs." See the Clery Project's public Web site, http://clergyproject.org/about-the-clergy-project/.

For more on depression and burnout among clergy, see Paul Vitello, "Taking a Break From the Lord's Work," *New York Times*, August 1, 2010, www.nytimes.com/2010/08/02/nyregion/02burnout.html?pagewanted=all&_r=0. See also "Clergy Healthy Initiative" on the Duke Divinity School Web site, http://divinity.duke.edu/initiatives-centers/clergy-health-initiative.

1. Living in Isolation
Dale McGowan, *Parenting Beyond Belief: On Raising Ethical Caring Children Without Religion* (New York: Amacom, 2007) and the Web site http://parentingbeyondbelief.com.

Video of Sam Harris presenting at the 2004 IdeaCity Conference is available on YouTube at www.youtube.com/watch?v=m5tGpMcFF7U. For more on his views, see Sam Harris,

The End of Faith (New York: W. W. Norton, 2004). For more on the the annual IdeaCity Conference, see www.ideacityonline.com.

Video of Daniel C. Dennett's talk at the 2010 Atheist Alliance International/Humanist Canada Convention in Montreal is available on YouTube at www.youtube.com/watch?v=m5tGpMcFF7U. Daniel Dennett and Linda LaScola's landmark study, "Preachers Who Are Not Believers," *Evolutionary Psychology* 8, no. 1 (March 2010): 122–150, is available at www.epjournal.net/wp-content/uploads/EP08122150.pdf

2. Making Things Happen

Details from author interviews and e-mail correspondence. All content used with permission.

Dan Barker, *Godless: How and Evangelical Preacher became one of America's Leading Atheists* (Berkeley: Ulysses Press, 2008).

For some of the media coverage the Clergy Project and its members have received, see Mike Aus's appearance on *Up with Chris Hayes*, March 25, 2012, www.nbcnews.com/video/up/46848396; Mary Hynes, *Tapestry*, "The Exit Ramp," April 26, 2013, www.cbc.ca/tapestry/episode/2013/04/26/the-exit-ramp/; and Mary Hynes, "Preachers Who Don't Believe in God," *Tapestry*, August 21, 2013, www.cbc.ca/tapestry/episode/2011/02/27/preachers-who-dont-believe-in-god/.

3. Going Live

All content used with permission.

4. Surveying the Numbers

To date, Daniel Dennett and Linda LaScola are the only researchers that have conducted a thorough qualitative study of nonbelieving clergy. Providing a view into the world of clergy and seminary students who have shed their belief, first in their study "Preachers Who Are Not Believers" and later in their book, *Caught in the Pulpit: Leaving Belief Behind*, exp. ed. (Durham, NC: Pitchstone Publishing, 2015), Dennett and LaScola challenge readers' thinking about life

in ministry. Their work, along with the emergence of the Clergy
Project, point to an emerging trend of declining religiosity that has
been observed in numerous studies.

Barbara G. Wheeler, Sharon L. Miller, and Daniel O. Aleshire,
*How Are We Doing? The Effectiveness of Theological Schools as Measured
by the Vocations and Views of Graduates* (Auburn Theological Seminary,
December 2007), www.auburnseminary.org/sites/default/files/
How%20are%20We%20Doing.pdf

Sociologists Alan S. Miller and Rodney Stark have argued that
differential socialization does not account for the differences in
levels of religiosity between males and females. See "Gender and
Religiousness: Can Socialization Explanations Be Saved?" *American
Journal of Sociology* 107, no. 6 (May 2002).

5. Thinking through Faith

At the time I was unaware of the Cerne Abbas Giant, a giant figure
with an erect penis cut into a hill outside Dorset, which offered
its own unique tableau for presumed heavenly viewers and may
have been created as a joke in the seventeenth century. Perhaps
knowledge of that particular landmark would not have made me so
proud of my church's design.

Though the focus of this book is not the eruption of sexual
abuse of minors by Roman Catholic clergy, the events that
transpired in my diocese and my parish played a pivotal role in my
emerging skepticism. Sexual abuse scandals have been a recurring
theme in the Roman Catholic Church since the early 1980s.

"Sylvia's Site" is a resource for those searching for information
regarding "the sex abuse scandal and betrayals of trust in the Roman
Catholic Church in Canada." For more information on Father
Claude Richard and his brother, Father Clair Richard, see www.
theinquiry.ca/wordpress/accused/charged/richard-father-claude-
richard/; www.theinquiry.ca/wordpress/accused/charged/richard-
father-clair-richard/; and www.theinquiry.ca/wordpress/accused/
charged/richard-father-claude-richard/r-v-richard-sentencing/.

For an article about the abuse at Mount Cashel Orphanage in

Newfoundland, see "Mount Cashel Abuse Settlement Sets Stage for More Suits," CBC News, May 24, 2013, www.cbc.ca/news/canada/newfoundland-labrador/mount-cashel-abuse-settlement-sets-stage-for-more-suits-1.1311548. For additional information about Mount Cashel, see http://en.wikipedia.org/wiki/Mount_Cashel_Orphanage.

For more on Bishop Campbell, see Daven Jeffrey, "Retired Bishop Campbell Dies," *Chronicle Herald*, January 18, 2012, http://thechronicleherald.ca/novascotia/53424-retired-bishop-campbell-dies; Allision Lawlor, "Nova Scotia Bishop's Opinions Were Often Controversial," *Globe and Mail*, February 7, 2012, http://v1.theglobeandmail.com/servlet/story/LAC.20120207.OBCOLINCAMPBELLATL/BDAStory/BDA/deaths.

For more on Bishop Lahey, see "Catholic Church Strips Raymond Lahey of Duties," CBC News, May 16, 2012, www.cbc.ca/news/canada/newfoundland-labrador/catholic-church-strips-raymond-lahey-of-duties-1.1192514.

The Casket (www.thecasket.ca) is a weekly paper published in Antigonish, Nova Scotia by Brace Publishing Limited, which acquired the independent newspaper in 2012. Prior to that, the majority stakeholder had been the Diocese of Antigonish.

Clifford Geertz, "Religion as a Cultural System," in *Anthropological Approaches to the Study of Religion*, ed. Michael Banton, pp. 1–46 (London: Tavistock Publications, 1966).

Quotations of Clergy Project members who have detailed their struggles with doubt come from Rational Doubt. See "Stan Bennett," "Clergy Doubt #10: He Tried His Damnedest to Believe and Now Wants Out," March 9, 2015, www.patheos.com/blogs/rationaldoubt/2015/03/1801/#ixzz3WpsWLJHW; Mary Johnson, "Clergy Doubt #5: Left Convent Life First, Then Religion," February 16, 2015, www.patheos.com/blogs/rationaldoubt/2015/02/clergy-doubt-5-left-convent-life-first-then-religion/#ixzz3X2hituYw; "Sherm," "Clergy Doubt #2: Doubt that Leads to Disbelief Doesn't Dissuade Orthodox Practice," February 15, 2015, www.patheos.com/blogs/rationaldoubt/2015/02/doubt-that-leads-to-disbeliefdoesnt-dissuade-orthodox-practice/#ixzz3X2i3j55y; and Mason Lane, "Clergy Doubt #1: Fundamentalism Isn't Fun," February 2, 2015, www.patheos.com/blogs/rationaldoubt/2015/02/clergy-doubt-1-fundamentalism-isnt-fun/#ixzz3WpuFLxGX.

For information on publications by Clergy Project founders and members, as well as by contributors to Rational Doubt, visit www.patheos.com/blogs/rationaldoubt/books/.

6. Driving Doubt: Seminary

Three studies published by the Center for the Study of Theological Education at Auburn Theological Seminary, a seminary for the Presbyterian Church, are especially relevant to this discussion: Barbara G. Wheeler, Anthony T. Ruger, and Sharon L. Miller, *Theological Student Enrollment: A Special Report from the Auburn Center for Study of Theological Education* (August 2013), www.auburnseminary.org/sites/default/files/Theological%20Student%20Enrollment-%20Final.pdf; Wheeler, Miller, and Aleshire, *How Are We Doing?*; and Barbara G. Wheeler, *Is There a Problem? Theological Students and Religious Leadership for the Future* (July 2001), www.auburnseminary.org/sites/default/files/Is%20There%20a%20Problem.pdf. These studies align with my experience concerning the challenges associated with attending seminary and the formation of clergy.

According to the Center for the Study of Theological Education Web site, "The Center for the Study of Theological Education (CSTE) provides reliable information and perspectives on theological education in North America. It conducts a 'cycle of surveys' that revisits segments of theological education—students, graduates, faculty, administrators, trustees, and seminary finances—regularly, in order to track trends over time. CSTE also studies special topics, such as student debt, doctoral education in theology and religion, and the culture of theological schools." See www.auburnseminary.org/research?par=838

Liberation theology was born out of the desire for social justice. The two pioneers of Latin American liberation theology are Leonardo Boff and Gustavo Gutierrez, both ordained priests whose emphasis on social justice for the poor raised many eyebrows in the Vatican. In 1985, in an interview with *Comunità Italiana*, Boff accused the Congregation on the Doctrine of Faith and specifically Cardinal Ratzinger of "religious terrorism." For further biographical information on Gutierrez and Boff, see http://en.wikipedia.org/ wiki/Gustavo_Guti%C3%A9rrez and http://en.wikipedia.org/ wiki/Leonardo_Boff, respectively.

Diarmuid O'Murchu, *Quantum Theology: Spiritual Implications of the New Physics* (New York: Crossroad Publishing Company, 1996). For a scientific critique of the problems with "quantum theology," see Victor J. Stenger, *Quantum Gods: Creation, Cosmos, and the Search for Cosmic Consciousness* (Amherst, NY: Prometheus Books, 2009).

For a background summary of Paul Tillich, see http:// en.wikipedia.org/wiki/Paul_Tillich. For a background summary of Bernard Lonergan, see http://en.wikipedia.org/wiki/Lonergan.

7. Deconstructing Religion: Feminism
For a short summary of the martyrdom of Perpetual and Felicity in 203 AD, see http://en.wikipedia.org/wiki/Perpetua_and_Felicity.

Key works by Mary Daly include *Beyond God the Father* (Boston: Beacon Press, 1985); "Radical Feminism," *Philosophy Now* no. 39 (October 2001): 15–18; and *The Church and the Second Sex* (Boston: Beacon Press, 1985).

For background information on Joanna Manning, see www. joannamanning.com/bio3.html.

Elizabeth Cady Stanton, *The Women's Bible* (New York: European Publishing, 1895).

8. Transforming Values: LGBT Rights
The passage about homosexuality in the Catechism of the Catholic Church, No. 2357, is available at www.vatican.va/archive/ccc_css/ archive/catechism/p3s2c2a6.htm.

Queer Theology, an emergent liberation theology, is pushing the church to expand its natural order to remove the requirement of procreation as a central tenet of human sexual morality. For more, see Patrick S. Cheng, *Radical Love: An Introduction to Queer Theology* (New York: Seabury Books, 2011); Robert Goss and Jay Johnson, "A 'Queer God'? Really? Remembering Marcella Althaus-Reid," Center for Lesbian and Gay Studies in Religion and Ministry, www.clgs.org/blog/commentary/queer-god-really-remembering-marcella-althaus-reid); and "Profile: Dr. Marcella Althaus-Reid," Religious Archives Network, www.lgbtran.org/Profile.aspx?ID=234 Background.

9. Searching for a New Calling
For more on the program to help members find secular employment, see http://clergyproject.org/transitional-assistance-grant/.

10. Developing New Communities
For more about Jerry DeWitt, see http://jerrydewitt.net/. For more about Houston Oasis, see www.houstonoasis.org.

11. Confronting Losses
For more on my situation with my mother, see Catherine Dunphy, "After Coming Out as an Atheist, I Was Shunned by My Mother," *Patheos*, Friendly Atheist blog, November 25, 2012, www.patheos.com/blogs/friendlyatheist/2013/11/25/after-coming-out-as-an-atheist-i-was-shunned-by-my-mother.

Mary Johnson, *An Unquenchable Thirst: A Memoir* (New York: Spiegel & Grau, 2013.)

12. Looking Ahead
For more on the increasing numbers of nones, see Tobin Grant, "7.5 Million People Left Religion Since 2012," Religion News Service, March 12, 2015, http://tobingrant.religionnews.com/2015/03/12/7-5-million-people-left-religion-since-2012-three-graphs-latest-general-social-survey/.

Appendix
The four sketches have not been previously published.

ABOUT THE AUTHOR

Catherine Dunphy is an original member of the Clergy Project and its former executive director. She is operations manager and contributor at Rational Doubt, a Patheos blog. Trained as a Roman Catholic chaplain, her journey out of faith began and ended while attending seminary. She was an atheist by the time she graduated with her Master of Theological Studies degree in 2004.